PRACTICE GUIDELINES
In Primary Care

Ralph Gonzales, MD, MSPH

Assistant Professor
Division of General Internal Medicine
Department of Medicine
University of Colorado Health Sciences Center
Denver, Colorado

Jean S. Kutner, MD, MSPH

Assistant Professor
Division of General Internal Medicine
Department of Medicine
University of Colorado Health Sciences Center
Denver, Colorado

Lange Medical Books/McGraw-Hill
Medical Publishing Division

New York   St. Louis   San Francisco   Auckland   Bogotá   Caracas
Lisbon   London   Madrid   Mexico City   Milan   Montreal
New Delhi   San Juan   Singapore   Sydney   Tokyo   Toronto

McGraw-Hill

A Division of The **McGraw·Hill** Companies

1 2 3 4 5 6 7 8 9 0 DOC DOC 0 9 8 7 6 5 4 3 2 1 0

ISBN 0-8385-3417-1
ISSN 1528-1612

Notice

Medicine is an ever-changing science. As new research and clinical experience broaden our knowledge, changes in treatment and drug therapy are required. The authors and the publisher of this work have checked with sources believed to be reliable in their efforts to provide information that is complete and generally in accord with the standards accepted at the time of publication. However, in view of the possibility of human error or changes in medical sciences, neither the authors nor the publisher nor any other party who has been involved in the preparation or publication of this work warrants that the information contained herein is in every respect accurate or complete, and they disclaim all responsibility for any errors or ommissions or for the results obtained from use of the information contained in this work. Readers are encouraged to confirm the information contained herein with other sources. For example and in particular, readers are advised to check the product information sheet included in the package of each drug they plan to administer to be certain that the information contained in this work is accurate and that changes have not been made in the recommended dose or in the contraindications for administration. This recommendation is of particular importance in connection with new or infrequently used drugs.

This book was set by Octal Publishing, Inc.

R. R. Donnelley & Sons, Inc. was printer and binder

Contents

DISEASE SCREENING

DISEASE PREVENTION

DISEASE MANAGEMENT: HEDIS© CONDITIONS, PERFORMANCE MEASURES, AND MANAGEMENT STRATEGIES

APPENDICES

Preface

PURPOSE

Practice Guidelines in Primary Care is intended for primary care clinicians. These include medical and nursing students during their ambulatory care rotations, registered nurses, nurse practitioners, and physician assistants; as well as residents and practicing physicians in the specialties of family medicine, internal medicine, pediatrics, and obstetrics and gynecology. Its purpose is to make recognized screening and primary prevention and treatment recommendations readily accessible and available for clinical decision making.

Recommendations relating to screening, prevention, evaluation, and treatment are issued regularly by governmental agencies, expert panels, medical specialty organizations, and other professional and scientific organizations. *Practice Guidelines in Primary Care* is essential for the busy clinician. Guidelines are continually being published by organizations that express different positions on the same topics, and current guidelines require revision as new evidence from clinical and outcomes research emerges. The intent of this guide is to help clinicians select the most appropriate clinical preventive services for a given situation.

CONTENT

A major focus of *Practice Guidelines in Primary Care* is screening and primary prevention, both of which apply only to persons without evidence of current disease. **Screening** encompasses tests or examinations intended to identify persons who require specific interventions. **Primary prevention** describes interventions intended to prevent the onset of particular conditions.

An effective screening test is one that detects a condition earlier than would be detected without screening and has sufficient accuracy to avoid producing large numbers of false-positive or false-negative results. Screening is appropriate only if this early detection improves health outcomes. To be considered effective, preventive interventions should decrease disease-specific morbidity or mortality.

We have also included disease management algorithms for some of the most common conditions managed by primary care clinicians. In our first edition, we have focused on those conditions that are of such paramount importance that the care for these conditions is annually reviewed by the National Committee for Quality Assurance in their accreditation of managed care organizations. Further, we have included the HEDIS© performance measures that are currently being used to evaluate managed care organizations and will likely be used more commonly in the future to provide feedback to individual clinicians.

Included in this guide are evidence-based recommendations from recognized medical specialty societies, other professional and scientific organizations, governmental health service entities, and the medical literature. A list of these organizations, along with their Internet addresses, is located in the Appendix.

We are grateful to the internal medicine house staff from New York University Medical Center and from the University of Colorado Health Sciences Center for providing valuable feedback.

Ralph Gonzales, MD, MSPH
Jean S. Kutner, MD, MSPH

Denver, Colorado
March 2000

1
Disease Screening

ALCOHOL ABUSE & DEPENDENCE

Disease Screening	Organization	Date	Population	Recommendations	Comments	Source
Alcohol Abuse & Dependence	GAPS AAP Bright Futures	1997 1995	Adolescents	Ask all adolescents annually about their use of alcohol. Parents should also routinely receive instructions on monitoring their adolescent's social and recreational activities for use of alcohol.[a]	The finding of alcohol use or abuse should provoke an assessment of other conditions that co-vary with alcohol abuse, such as cigarette smoking, sexual activity, and mood disorders. Guidelines on treatment of alcohol abuse in adolescence have been published. (*J Am Acad Child Adolesc Psychiatry* 1998;37:122)	*Arch Pediatr Adolesc Med* 1997;151:123 *Pediatrics* 1995;95:439
	USPSTF CTF	1996 1994	Adolescents and adults	Screen all adolescents and adults using relevant history or a standardized screening instrument (see Appendix I).	The simplest, most widely used screening instrument is the CAGE questionnaire, which has a sensitivity of 74% and specificity of 79% (*JAMA* 1984;252:1905)	
	ACOG AAP	1997	Pregnant women	Counsel all pregnant women regarding the maternal health and fetal effects of alcohol during pregnancy.		AAP and ACOG: Guidelines for Perinatal Care, 4th ed. ACOG, 1997.

[a]The AAP also acknowledges the importance of family attitudes toward alcohol and recommends that clinicians urge parents to use alcohol safely and in moderation, to restrict children from family alcohol supplies, and to recognize the influence their own drinking patterns can have on their children and parenting.

ANEMIA

Disease Screening	Organization	Date	Population	Recommendations	Comments	Source
Anemia, Iron-Deficient	AAP	1993	Neonates	Universal hematocrit screening is not recommended.		Pediatrics 1993;92:474
	AAFP	1997	Infants ages 6–12 months	Perform selective, single hemoglobin or hematocrit screening for high-risk infants. [a]		
	USPSTF	1996				
	USPSTF	1996	Pregnant women	Screen all women with hemoglobin or hematocrit at first prenatal visit.		

[a]Includes infants living in poverty, blacks, Native Americans and Alaska Natives, immigrants from developing countries, preterm and low birth weight infants, and infants whose principal dietary intake is unfortified cow's milk.

CANCER, BLADDER

Disease Screening	Organization	Date	Population	Recommendations	Comments	Source
Cancer, Bladder	AAFP USPSTF CTF	1997 1996 1994	Asymptomatic persons[a]	Routine screening with microscopic urinalysis, urine dipstick, or urine cytology is not recommended.	Positive predictive value of serial dipstick screening for malignancy: 6–8% (USPSTF). Dipstick testing is sensitive and specific for hematuria, but hematuria is not specific for bladder cancer.	www.aafp.org/ exam/app-d_c.html

[a]Increased risk: exposure to azodyes, aromatic amines, and 4-aminobiphenyl; employment in the leather, tire, or rubber industries; and cigarette smoking (OR/RR 1.5–7.0). Persons working in high-risk professions may be eligible for screening at the worksite, although the benefit of this has not been determined. People who smoke should be advised that smoking significantly increases the risk for bladder cancer, and all smokers should be routinely counseled to quit smoking. A high index of suspicion should be maintained in anyone with a history of smoking or exposure to another risk factor. (USPSTF)

CANCER, BREAST						
Disease Screening	Organization	Date	Population[a]	Recommendations	Comments	Source
Cancer, Breast	ACS	1998	Women age ≥ 20 years	Monthly BSE	The value of BSE in reducing breast cancer mortality remains unproved. (Br J Cancer 1993;68:208) BSE is considered supplemental to, rather than a substitute for, screening by CBE and mammography.	www.cancer.org/ guide/ guidchec.html
	ACS ACOG	1998	Women ages 20– 40 years	CBE every 3 years		www.cancer.org/ guide/ guidchec.html www.acog.org
	ACS ACOG	1998 1996	Women age ≥ 40 years	Mammography and CBE yearly		www.cancer.org/ guide/ guidchec.html www.acog.org
	NCI AMA	1999 1989	Women ages 40– 49 years	Mammography every 1–2 years and CBE yearly		cancernet.nci.nih.gov /clnpdq/screening JAMA 1989;261(17):2535

CANCER, BREAST

Disease Screening	Organization	Date	Population[a]	Recommendations	Comments	Source
Cancer, Breast (continued)	NIH AAFP	1997 1997	Women ages 40–49 years	Counsel about risks/benefits of mammography and CBE.	Extending screening to include ages 40–49 improves life expectancy by 2.5 days at a cost of $676/woman. Incremental cost-effectiveness is $105,000 per year of life saved. (Ann Intern Med 1997;127: 955) RCTs consistently demonstrate no benefit from screening in the first 5–7 years after study entry. At 10–12 years, benefit is uncertain. (J Natl Cancer Inst 1993;85(20):1644)Number needed to screen to save 1 life = 2500. (J Natl Cancer Inst 1997;89(14):1015) Thirty percent of all women screened annually at ages 40–49 will have at least 1 false-positive mammogram. (J Natl Cancer Inst 1997;22:139) Risk-based recommendations may assist in counseling. (J Clin Oncol 1998;16(9):3105)	NIH Consens Statement 1997;15(1):1 J Natl Cancer Inst 1997;89(14):1015 www.aafp.org/exam/app-d_c.html

CANCER, BREAST

Disease Screening	Organization	Date	Population[a]	Recommendations	Comments	Source
Cancer, Breast (continued)	NCI CTF ACP AMA	1999 1994 1991 1989	Women ages 50–69 years	Mammography and CBE yearly	For women ages 50–69, all studies show mortality reductions with screening of about 30% at 10–12 years. (J Natl Cancer Inst 1993;85(20):1644) Screening women ages 50–69 years improves life expectancy by 12 days at a cost of $704/woman, with a cost-effectiveness ratio of $21,400 per year of life saved. (Ann Intern Med 1997;127:955)	cancernet.nci.nih.gov /clinpdq/screening JAMA 1989;261(17):2535 Common Screening Tests. ACP, 1991.
	AAFP ACPM USPSTF	1997 1996 1996	Women ages 50–69 years	Mammography and CBE every 1–2 years		www.aafp.org/exam/ app-d_c/html www.acpm.org/ breast.htm
	ACPM USPSTF AGS	1996 1996 1989	Women age ≥ 70 years	Mammography and CBE every 1–2 years AGS recommends, in addition, monthly BSE.	Currently available data for women age ≥ 70 are inadequate to judge the effectiveness of screening. (J Natl Cancer Inst 1993;85(20):1644)	www.acpm.org/ breast.htm J Am Geriatr Soc 1989;37(9):883

[a] Women with a mother and sister with breast cancer have an RR > 4.0 of developing breast cancer. It is likely that < 10% of all breast cancer in western countries is attributable to genetic predisposition. It has been estimated that 25% of breast cancers diagnosed before age 40 years are attributable to *BRCA1* mutations. Studies have not addressed when to begin breast cancer screening, and at what intervals, for women at high risk of breast cancer because of genetic predisposition. (Annu Rev Public Health 1996;17:47)

CANCER, CERVICAL						
Disease Screening	**Organization**	**Date**	**Population**	**Recommendations[a]**	**Comments**	**Source**
Cancer, Cervical	NCI ACS ACOG GAPS Bright Futures	1999 1998 1998 1994 1994	Women who are or have been sexually active Or Women age ≥ 18 years[b]	Pap smear (with endocervical brush and spatula) and pelvic exam every year: if ≥ 3 consecutive normal exams, may perform less frequently at physician discretion	Lead time from precancerous lesions to invasive cancer is 8–9 years. (Clinician's Handbook of Preventive Services. US Government Printing Office, 1994) Single screening Pap test for detecting CIN grades I and II has sensitivity 14–99%, specificity 24–96%. (Am J Epidemiol 1995;141:680) 20–60% reduction in cervical cancer mortality rates after implementation of screening programs (Ann Intern Med 1990;113(3):214)	www.cancer.org/guide/guidclhec.html cancernet.nci.nih.giv/clinpdq/screening www.acog.org Can Med Assoc J 1991;144:313
	AAFP USPSTF ACP	1997 1996 1990	Women who have ever had sex and have a cervix[b]	Pap smear at least every 3 years		www.aafp.org/app-d_c.html Ann Intern Med 1990;113(3):214

Disease Screening	Organization	Date	Population	Recommendations[a]	Comments	Source
Cancer, Cervical (continued)	ACPM CTF	1996 1994	Women who have ever had sex[b]	Pap smear every year for 2 years; if 2 normal annual smears, lengthen screening interval to 3 years at physician discretion		www.acpm.org/cervical.htm
	ACPM USPSTF	1996 1996	Women age ≥ 65 years	Discontinue screening if: regular screening, 2 satisfactory smears, and no abnormal smears within previous 9 years. If no previous screening, 3 normal smears before discontinuation	28–64% of women age ≥ 65 have never had a Pap smear or have not had one done within 3 years. (Mt Sinai J Med 1985;52:284)	www.acpm.org/cervical.htm
	CTF AGS	1994 1993	Women age ≥ 65 years	Pap smear every 3 years until age 70. If no or insufficient prior Pap smears, 2 annual smears before discontinuation.		www.americangeriatrics.org/positionpapers/cerc–car.html

[a]Risk factors for cervical cancer: sexual activity, early onset of sexual intercourse, history of multiple sexual partners, history of STDs (especially HPV/HIV), smoking, and no previous screening (may indicate more frequent screening interval). (http://www.cancernet.nci.gov/clinpdq/screening; Ann Intern Med 1990;113(3):214) Cervical cancer is causally related to infection with HPV. (http://odp.od.nih.gov/consensus/)

[b]If sexual history is unknown or considered unreliable, screening should begin at age 18 years.

Disease Screening	Organization	Date	Population	Recommendations	Comments	Source
CANCER, COLORECTAL						
Cancer, Colorectal	ASCRS	1992	Age ≥ 40 years Age ≥ 50 years	Yearly DRE and FOBT[a] Flexible sigmoidoscopy every 3-5 years	Models indicate that screening persons > 50 years for colorectal cancer with annual FOBT, flexible sigmoidoscopy, or a single colonoscopy compares favorably with screening mammography in women age > 50 years in the cost per year of life saved. (N Engl J Med 1995;332(13);861)	www.fascrs.org/ascrspp-docn.html
	NCI	1999	Ages 50-80 years	Guaiac-based FOBT every 1-2 years Regular screening by flexible sigmoidoscopy may decrease mortality from colon cancer. There is insufficient evidence to determine optimal interval.	Annual FOBT decreased 13-year cumulative mortality by 13% (vs 6% with biennial FOBT). (N Engl J Med 1993;19(328):1365) U.S. military veterans who did not have colorectal cancer were 50% more likely to have had endoscopic procedures. (Ann Intern Med 1995;123:904)	cancernet.cni.nih.gov/clinpdq/screening/

Disease Screening	Organization	Date	Population	Recommendations	Comments	Source
Cancer, Colorectal (continued)	ACS AGA AAFP	1997	Age ≥ 50 years[b]	Yearly FOBT and flexible sigmoidoscopy and DRE every 5 years[a] Or Colonoscopy + DRE every 10 years Or Double contrast BE + DRE every 5–10 years		www.cancer.org/ guide/ guidehec.html www.gastrology/ colcancer www.aafp.org/ app-exam/app-d_c.html
	ACP	1997	Ages 50–70 years	Yearly FOBT[a] and flexible sigmoidoscopy; colonoscopy; or air contrast BE every 10 years		www.acponline. org/journals/ annals/ 15may97/ ppcolo1.htm
	USPSTF	1996	Age ≥ 50 years[b]	Yearly FOBT Or Flexible sigmoidoscopy (no periodicity), or both There is insufficient evidence to recommend for or against DRE, BE, or colonoscopy.		

CANCER, COLORECTAL

CANCER, COLORECTAL

[a] A positive result on an FOBT should be followed by a complete colorectal exam by colonoscopy. An alternative is flexible sigmoidoscopy and air-contrast BE. (Ann Intern Med 1997;126(10):808, http:www.gastro.org/colcancer)

[b] Risk factors indicating need for earlier/more frequent screening: personal history of colorectal cancer or adenomatous polyps, colorectal cancer or polyps in a first-degree relative < 60 years old or in a second-degree relative of any age, personal history of chronic inflammatory bowel disease, and family with hereditary colorectal cancer syndromes. (Ann Intern Med 1998;128(1):900, N Engl J Med 1994;331(25):1669, N Engl J Med 1995;332(13):861)

CANCER, ENDOMETRIAL

Disease Screening	Organization	Date	Population	Recommendations	Comments	Source
Cancer, Endometrial	NCI	1999	All women	Routine screening of women for endometrial cancer is not recommended.	Presence of endometrial cells in Pap test from postmenopausal woman not taking exogenous hormones is abnormal and requires further evaluation. Endometrial thickness of < 4 mm on transvaginal ultrasound is associated with low risk of endometrial cancer. (Obstet Gynecol 1991;78(2):195)	cancernet.nci.nih. gov/clinpdq
	ACS	1998	All postmenopausal women	Selective screening with endometrial tissue sampling when menopause begins for high-risk women[a]		www.cancer.org/ guide/guidehec/ html

[a]Increased endometrial cancer risk: history of infertility, obesity, previous abnormal uterine bleeding, estrogen therapy unopposed by progestin intake, tamoxifen therapy, and genetic mutations associated with hereditary nonpolyposis colon cancer. (Obstet Gynecol 1999;93(4):594, http://cancernet.nci.nih.gov/clinpdq)

Disease Screening	Organization	Date	Population	Recommendations	Comments	Source
	CANCER, GASTRIC					**CANCER, LIVER**
Cancer, Gastric	NCI	1999	Adults in United States	Routine screening of the US population is not recommended.	Studies of screening in Japan (via barium x-ray) have demonstrated decreases in mortality in screened versus unscreened patients. (Int J Cancer 1995;60:45)	cancernet.nci.nih.gov/clinpdq
Cancer, Liver (Hepatocellular Carcinoma)	Workshop on Screening for Hepatocellular Cancer (Indian Health Service, Fox Chase Cancer Center, CDC)	1989	High-risk children and adults[a]	HBsAg-positive carriers: α-fetoprotein level at least annually, preferably twice a year
HBsAg-positive carriers with cirrhosis or family history of HCC: periodic ultrasound and α-fetoprotein
HBsAg negative with cirrhosis or chronic liver disease: no screening recommendations		J Natl Cancer Inst 1991;83:916
MMWR 1990;39:619

[a]The incidence of HCC is high in persons positive for HBsAg for ≥ 6 months. Especially high risk: males, cirrhosis, age > 45 years, and family history of HCC. (J Natl Cancer Inst 1991;83:916, Arch Intern Med 1989;149:1741)

Disease Screening	Organization	Date	Population	Recommendations	Comments	Source
Cancer, Lung	NCI AAFP USPSTF CTF ACS ACP ATS ACR	1999 1997 1996 1994 1993 1991 1983 1982	Asymptomatic persons	Routine screening for lung cancer with chest radiography or sputum cytology is not recommended.	All patients should be counseled against tobacco use. No significant benefit in terms of lung cancer mortality by screening with chest radiography and sputum cytology. (J Occup Med 1986;28:746) Annual low-dose chest CT in high-risk patients appears to increase detection of resectable cancer. Impact of screening on mortality has not been determined. (Lancet 1999;354(9173):99)	cancernet.nci.nih.gov/clinpdq/screening www.aafp.org/exam/app-d_c.html www.cancer.org/guide/ guidchec.html Common Screening Tests. ACP, 1991. Am Rev Respir Dis 1984;130:565 www.acr.org
Cancer, Oral	NCI USPSTF CTF	1999 1996 1994	Asymptomatic persons	Insufficient evidence to recommend for or against routine screening		cancernet.nci.nih.gov/clinpdq/screening

CANCER, ORAL

Disease Screening	Organization	Date	Population	Recommendations	Comments	Source
Cancer, Oral (continued)	NIDR	1994	Asymptomatic persons	Screen during routine dental exam.		Detecting Oral Cancer: A Guide for Dentists. NIDR, 1994.
	USPSTF CTF	1996 1994	High-risk persons[a]	Consider annual oral exam. [b]		
	ACS	1993	Ages 20–40 years	Screen with oral exam (inspection and palpation of oral cavity) every 3 years.		www.cancer.org/ guide/ guidchec.html
	ACS	1993	Age > 40 years	Screen with annual oral exam.		www.cancer.org/ guide/ guidchec.html
	AGS	1991	Age ≥ 60 years	Screen with annual oral exam.		J Am Geriatr Soc 1991;39(9):920

[a]Risk factors: regular alcohol or tobacco use.
[b]Inquire about alcohol and tobacco use and counsel about risk.

	CANCER, OVARIAN			

Disease Screening	Organization	Date	Population	Recommendations	Comments	Source
Cancer, Ovarian	NCI ACPM USPSTF AAFP ACP CTF	1999 1997 1996 1996 1994 1994	Asymptomatic women[a]	Screening with ultrasound, serum tumor markers, or pelvic exam is not recommended.	In asymptomatic women, pelvic exam has unknown sensitivity and specificity; abdominal ultrasound has specificity 97.7%, sensitivity 100%, positive predictive value 2.6%; transvaginal ultrasound has specificity 98.1%, sensitivity 100%, positive predictive value 22%; CA-125 has sensitivity 50% for stages I and II and 90% for stages III and IV, and specificity 97.6%, when followed by abdominal ultrasound. (Ann Intern Med 1993;118(11):838, http://www.acpm.org/ovary.htm)	www.cancernet.nci.nih.gov/clinpdq/screening www.acpm.org/ovary.htm www.aafp.org/exam/app-d_c.html Ann Intern Med 1994;121(2):124
	NIH	1994	Asymptomatic women[a]	Comprehensive family history and annual rectovaginal pelvic exam		NIH Consens Statement 1994;12(3):1

[a]Risk factors: age > 60 years; low parity; personal history of endometrial, colon, or breast cancer; family history of ovarian cancer; and hereditary ovarian cancer syndrome. Lifetime risk of ovarian cancer in a woman with no affected relatives is 1 in 70. If 1 first-degree relative has ovarian cancer, lifetime risk is 5%. If 2 or more first-degree relatives have ovarian cancer, lifetime risk is 7%. Women with 2 or more family members affected by ovarian cancer have a 3% chance of having a hereditary ovarian cancer syndrome. These women have a 40% lifetime risk of ovarian cancer. There are no data demonstrating that screening high-risk women reduces their mortality from ovarian cancer. A low annual incidence (13.8/100,000) means that many people must be screened to find only a few cases of disease. (NIH Consens Statement 1994;12(3):1, Am Intern Med 1993;118(11):838)

Disease Screening	Organization	Date	Population	Recommendations	Comments	Source
CANCER, PANCREATIC						
Cancer, Pancreatic	USPSTF CTF	1996 1994	Asymptomatic persons	Routine screening using abdominal palpation, ultrasonography, or serologic markers is not recommended.	Cigarette smoking has consistently been associated with increased risk of pancreatic cancer.	
CANCER, PROSTATE						
Cancer, Prostate	NCI	1999	Asymptomatic men	Insufficient evidence to establish whether a decrease in mortality from prostate cancer occurs with screening by DRE, TRUS, or PSA		cancernet.nci.nih.gov/clinpdy/screening
	ACS AUA	1998 1997	Men age ≥ 50 years[a]	Offer annual PSA and DRE if ≥ 10-year life expectancy.[b]	DRE has sensitivity 50%, specificity 94%, PSA has sensitivity 67%, specificity 84%. TRUS has sensitivity 81%, specificity 84%. (JAMA 1994;272(10):773)	www.cancer.org/guide/guidchec.html auanet.org/pub_pat/policies/uroservices.html

Disease Screening	Organization	Date	Population	Recommendations	Comments	Source
Cancer, Prostate (continued)	ACPM ACP AAFP	1998 1997 1997	Men age ≥ 50 years[a]	Describe potential benefits and known harms of screening with PSA and DRE, diagnosis, and treatment; listen to the patient's concerns; and individualize the decision to screen.[c]	DRE and PSA measurement might be cost-effective for men ages 50–69 years when compared with estimates for other screening methods. (Ann Intern Med 1997;126(6):468)	www.acpm.org/ prostate.htm Ann Intern Med 1997;126(6):480 www.aafp.org/exam/ app-d_c.html
	USPSTF	1996	Men age ≥ 50 years[a]	Routine screening with DRE, PSA, or TRUS is not recommended.		
	CTF	1994	Men age ≥ 50 years[a]	Poor evidence to include or exclude DRE, insufficient evidence to include PSA, and fair evidence to exclude TRUS		

[a] Men in high-risk groups (2 or more affected first-degree relatives, blacks) should begin screening at a younger age (eg, 45 years). More data on the precise age to start prostate cancer screening are needed for men at high risk. No direct or indirect evidence quantifies the yield and predictive value of early detection efforts in higher risk men. (http://www.cancer.org/guide/cebtec.html, http://aaanet.org/pub_pat/policies/uroservices.html, Ann Intern Med 1997;126(6):480)

[b] Some elevations in PSA may be due to benign conditions of the prostate. The DRE should be performed by health care workers skilled in recognizing subtle prostate abnormalities, including those of symmetry and consistency, as well as the more classic findings of marked induration or nodules. DRE is less effective in detecting prostate carcinoma than is PSA. (http://www.cancer.org/guide/guidehec.html, http://aaanet.org/pub_pat/policies/uroservices.html)

[c] Data are not yet available to quantify the risks and benefits of screening for prostate cancer or to prove that treating clinically localized cancer reduces disease-specific mortality rates. (Ann Intern Med 1997;126(6):468)

Disease Screening	Organization	Date	Population	Recommendations	Comments	Source
CANCER, SKIN						
Cancer, Skin	NCI USPSTF CTF	1999 1996 1994	Asymptomatic persons	Insufficient evidence to recommend for or against routine screening using total-body skin exam[a] Insufficient evidence to recommend for or against counseling patients to perform periodic skin self-exam[b]		cancernet.nci.nih.gov/clinpdq/screening
	NIH AAD	1992 1992	Asymptomatic persons	Annual screening using total-body skin exam		JAMA 1992;268(10):1314 J Am Acad Dermatol 1992;26:629
	ACS	1992	Ages 20–40 years	Screening with skin exam every 3 years		www.cancer.org/guide/guidchec.html

CANCER, SKIN

Disease Screening	Organization	Date	Population	Recommendations	Comments	Source
Cancer, Skin (continued)	ACS	1992	Age > 40 years	Annual screening with skin exam		www.cancer.org/ guide/ guidchec.html
	ACPM	1998	High-risk persons[a]	Periodic total skin exams		www.acpm.org/ skincanc.htm

[a]Clinicians should remain alert for skin lesions with malignant features when examining patients for other reasons, particularly patients with established risk factors. Risk factors for skin cancer include: evidence of melanocytic precursors, large numbers of common moles, immunosuppression, family or personal history of skin cancer, substantial cumulative lifetime sun exposure, intermittent intense sun exposure or severe sunburns in childhood, freckles, poor tanning ability, and light skin, hair, and eye color. Appropriate biopsy specimens should be taken of suspicious lesions. Persons with melanocytic precursor or marker lesions are at substantially increased risk for malignant melanoma and should be referred to skin cancer specialists for evaluation and surveillance. (USPSTF)

[b]Consider educating patients with established risk factors for skin cancer (see above) concerning signs and symptoms suggesting skin cancer and the possible benefits of periodic self-exam. (USPSTF)

CANCER, TESTICULAR

Disease Screening	Organization	Date	Population	Recommendations	Comments	Source
Cancer, Testicular	NCI USPSTF CTF	1999 1996 1994	Asymptomatic men[a]	Insufficient evidence to recommend for or against routine screening by physician exam, patient self-exam, or tumor markers (α-fetoprotein, human chorionic gonadotropin)		cancernet.nci.nih.gov/clinpdq/screening

[a]Patients with history of cryptorchidism, orchiopexy, or testicular atrophy should be informed of their increased risk for developing testicular cancer and counseled about screening. Such patients may then elect to be screened or to perform testicular self-exam. Adolescent and young adult males should be advised to seek prompt medical attention if they notice a scrotal abnormality. (USPSTF)

CANCER, THYROID

Disease Screening	Organization	Date	Population	Recommendations	Comments	Source
Cancer, Thyroid	AAFP USPSTF CTF	1997 1996 1994	Asymptomatic persons	Screening asymptomatic adults or children using either neck palpation or ultrasonography is not recommended.[a]	Neck palpation for nodules in asymptomatic individuals has sensitivity 15–38%; specificity 93–100%. Only a small proportion of nodular thyroid glands are neoplastic, resulting in a high-false positive rate. (USPSTF)	www.aafp.org/exam/app-d_c.html

[a]Includes asymptomatic persons with a history of external upper-body irradiation in infancy or childhood.

CARTOID ARTERY STENOSIS

Disease Screening	Organization	Date	Population	Recommendations	Comments	Source
Carotid Artery Stenosis (asymptomatic)	AHA	1998	Ages 40–79 years	Screen asymptomatic patients (? interval) with ≤ 5% surgical risk and ≥ 5-year life expectancy.[a]	In the Asymptomatic Carotid Atherosclerosis Study, the actuarial 5-year risk of ipsilateral stroke, operative stroke, and death was ≈ 5% with CEA vs 11% in the control group. Combined surgical morbidity and mortality was 2.3%. (JAMA 1995;273:1421)	www.americanheart.org/Scientific/statements/1998/029801.html
	CNS	1997	Ages 40–79 years	Insufficient evidence to screen asymptomatic individuals because CEA recommendation is "uncertain" for > 60% stenosis[b]		Can Med Assoc J 1997;157:653
	USPSTF	1996	Age > 60 years	Selective screening[c]		
	CTF	1994		Insufficient evidence to screen		
	SVS	1992		Selective screening[d]		J Vasc Surg 1992;15:469

CARTOID ARTERY STENOSIS

[a] If surgical risk is < 3% and life expectancy is ≥ 5 years, ipsilateral CEA is acceptable for ≥ 60% stenosis; if surgical risk is 3–5%, ipsilateral CEA is acceptable (but not proved) for ≥ 75% bilateral stenoses.

[b] Recommend stenosis be documented with angiography using the method of the North American Symptomatic Carotid Endarterectomy Trial.

[c] Selective screening may be appropriate in the presence of other stroke risk factors, no contraindications to major surgery, and access to surgeons and centers with < 3% perioperative morbidity and mortality.

[d] Screen patients with audible carotid bruit, multiple risk factors for CAS, or those who are preparing for operation in another vascular bed using duplex scan. Recommend CEA for patients with ≥ 75% stenosis with life expectancy ≥ 5 years and surgical risk < 3%. Other candidates for CEA include those with CT scan evidence of silent embolization, mixed plaque consistency, or evidence that the lesion has progressed over 6 months.

CHILD ABUSE & NEGLECT

Disease Screening	Organization	Date	Population	Recommendations	Comments	Source
Child Abuse & Neglect	GAPS	1997	Children and adolescents	All teens should be asked annually about a history of emotional, physical, and sexual abuse.	By law, child abuse must be reported to appropriate authorities in all 50 states.	Arch Pediatr Adolesc Med 1997;151:123

CHOLESTEROL & LIPID DISORDERS, CHILDREN

Disease Screening	Organization	Date	Population	Recommendations	Comments	Source
Cholesterol & Lipid Disorders, Children	USPSTF	1996	Children and adolescents	Insufficient evidence to recommend for or against screening		
	GAPS	1994	Age > 2 years	See AAP/NCEP recommendations; measure cholesterol only once if normal.		
	AAP/NCEP	1992	Age > 2 years	Selective screening[a] every 5 years if normal[b] Fasting lipids if strong family history Random total cholesterol if a parent has total cholesterol > 240 mg/dL. Clinician discretion (random total cholesterol) if unknown family history or presence of risk factors	Recommend pharmacologic treatment (eg, cholestyramine or cholestipol) if: (1) age > 10 years, on dietary therapy, and LDL > 190 mg/dL without other risk factors; or (2) LDL > 160 mg/dL and strong family history or 2 or more risk factors are present.[a]	Pediatrics 1992;89:525 Pediatrics 1992;90:469

CHOLESTEROL & LIPID DISORDERS, ADULTS

Disease Screening	Organization	Date	Population	Recommendations	Comments	Source
Cholesterol & Lipid Disorders, Adults	USPSTF	1996	Men ages 35–65 years Women ages 45–65 years	Random total cholesterol, periodicity based on risk factors; appropriate interval not known	Base treatment decisions on at least 2 cholesterol levels.	
			Men and women ages 66–75 years	Selective screening of older individuals with major CHD risk factors (hypertension, smoking, diabetes)		
			Men and women age > 75 years	Cholesterol screening not recommended		

CHOLESTEROL & LIPID DISORDERS, ADULTS

Disease Screening	Organization	Date	Population	Recommendations	Comments	Source
Cholesterol & Lipid Disorders, Adults (continued)	ACP	1996	Men age < 35 years Women age < 45 years	Screening not recommended unless history or physical exam suggests familial lipoprotein disorder, or at least 2 other CHD risk factors are present	Recommendations were published before 2 large primary prevention trials with HMG-CoA reductase inhibitors demonstrated efficacy and safety. (Lancet 1994;344:1383; N Engl J Med 1995;333:1301) Base treatment decisions on at least 2 cholesterol levels.	Ann Intern Med 1996;124:515
			Men ages 35-65 years Women ages 45-65 years	"Appropriate but not mandatory"; random total cholesterol every 5 years if normal		
			Men and women ages 66-75 years	Insufficient evidence to recommend for or against screening		
			Men and women age >75 years	Screening not recommended		

CHOLESTEROL & LIPID DISORDERS, ADULTS

Disease Screening	Organization	Date	Population	Recommendations	Comments	Source
Cholesterol & Lipid Disorders, Adults (continued)	AHA NCEP II	1996 1994	Men and women age ≥ 20 years	Check random HDL and total cholesterol every 5 years if desirable; otherwise see below.[b]		Circulation 1996;93:1067 JAMA 1993;269:3015 Circulation 1994;89:1329

[a] AAP and NCEP recommend annual screening if strong family history (parents or grandparents) of cardiovascular events at or before age 55 years (MI, positive coronary angiogram, stroke, or peripheral vascular disease) or presence of "several" risk factors (cigarette smoking, hypertension, obesity, diabetes, lack of physical activity).

[b] Classify TC < 200 mg/dL as desirable, 200–239 mg/dL as borderline, or ≥ 240 mg/dL as high.

1. If TC < 200 mg/dL and HDL ≥ 35 mg/dL, then repeat in 5 years; if TC < 200 mg/dL and HDL ≤ 35 mg/dL, then check fasting lipids and risk stratify (see Appendix VII).

2. If TC 200–239 mg/dL and HDL ≥ 35 mg/dL, then encourage behavior modifications and repeat lipids in 1–2 years; if TC 200–239 mg/dL and HDL ≤ 35 mg/ dL, then check fasting lipids and risk stratify.

3. If TC > 239 mg/dL, then check fasting lipids and risk stratify.

DEMENTIA						
Disease Screening	Organization	Date	Population	Recommendations	Comments	Source
Dementia	AHCPR	1996	Elderly	Perform selective screening[a] using a standardized instrument to assess cognitive function (see Appendix 1).[b]	Screening instruments are useful for detecting multiple cognitive deficits and determining a baseline for future assessments. Reversible causes of dementia include vitamin B_{12} deficiency, neurosyphilis, and hypothyroidism. The additional benefit of identifying early dementia is to prepare family for future patient needs.	Ann Intern Med 1988;19:70 J Am Geriatr Soc 1988;37:562 Activities of daily living: J Am Geriatr Soc 1985;33:698 Mini-Mental Status Exam: J Psychiatr Res 1975;12:189
	USPSTF CTF	1996 1994	Elderly	Insufficient evidence to recommend for or against screening asymptomatic persons	Remain alert for signs of declining cognitive function.[a] Be aware of other causes of mental status changes, such as depression, delirium, medication effects, and coexisting illnesses.	

[a]Triggers that should initiate an assessment for dementia include difficulties in (1) learning and retaining new information, (2) handling complex tasks (eg, balancing a checkbook or cooking a meal), (3) reasoning ability (eg, a new disregard for social norms), (4) spatial ability and orientation (eg, difficulty driving or getting lost), (5) language (eg, difficulties in word-finding), and (6) behavior (eg, appearing more passive or more irritable than usual).

[b]DSM IV diagnosis of dementia requires: (1) evidence of decline in functional abilities and (2) evidence of multiple cognitive deficiencies

Disease Screening	Organization	Date	Population	Recommendations	Comments	Source
					DEPRESSION	
Depression	GAPS Bright Futures	1994 1994	Adolescents	Annual screening for behaviors or emotions that might indicate depression or risk of suicide	Clues to depression include poor school performance, alcohol or drug use, and deteriorating parental or peer relationships. Clues to suicide risk include family dysfunction, physical and sexual abuse, substance abuse, history of recurrent or severe depression, and prior suicide attempt or plans.[a]	
	USPSTF	1996	Adults	Insufficient evidence to recommend for or against screening		
	AHCPR	1993	Adults	Selective screening when risk factors are present[b][c]	See screening instruments (Geriatric Depression Scale, Beck Depression Inventory— Short Form, PRIME-MD) in Appendix 1.	Clinical Practice Guideline No. 5: Depression in Primary Care. Agency for Healthcare Policy and Research; 1993. AHCPR Publication 93-0550 Arch Gen Psychiatry 1998;55:1121

[a]Suicide risk increases as the number of conditions increases. Parents of adolescents at risk for suicide should reduce access to firearms, weapons, or potentially lethal drugs in the home.

[b]Risk factors include prior episodes of depression, family history (first-degree relative) of depressive disorder, prior suicide attempts, age < 40 years, female gender, postpartum period, medical comorbidity, lack of social support, stressful life events, and current alcohol or substance abuse.

[c]Suspicion or documentation of depression by history should lead to a mental status exam that includes documentation of suicidal ideation; level of orientation, alertness, cooperation, and communication; level of motor activity; and presence or absence of psychotic features.

DIABETES MELLITUS						
Disease Screening	Organization	Date	Population	Recommendations	Comments	Source
Diabetes Mellitus, Gestational	ADA	1998	Pregnant women age ≥ 25 years or high risk[a]	Screening test: 1-hour OGTT at 24–28 weeks of gestation	Positive 1-hour OGTT: serum glucose ≥ 140 mg/dL after 50 g oral glucose Confirmation test: 3-hour OGTT	Diabetes Care 1998;21(suppl 1):1
	ACOG and AAP	1997	Pregnant women	Universal or selective screening at 24–28 weeks of gestation[b]		See Appendix IX
	USPSTF CTF	1996 1994	Pregnant women	Insufficient evidence to support screening	No evidence that universal screening results in meaningful clinical outcomes	
Diabetes Mellitus, Type 1	ADA	1998	Children and adults	Screening of any population is discouraged outside the context of defined research studies. High-risk individuals (first-degree relatives of type 1 diabetic patients) should be screened with immune-related markers, provided that positive patients are referred to appropriate study sites.		Diabetes Care 1998;21(suppl 1):1

Disease Screening	**Organization**	**Date**	**Population**	**Recommendations**	**Comments**	**Source**
Diabetes Mellitus, Type 2	ADA	1998	Adults	Selective screening of high-risk adults with fasting glucose[c]	Positive test: fasting serum glucose ≥ 126 mg/dL on 2 separate occasions. Screening appears to be more cost-effective for younger people (ages 25–45 years) and blacks.	Diabetes Care 1998;21(suppl 1):1 JAMA 1998;280:1757
	USPSTF	1996	Adults	Insufficient evidence to support screening asymptomatic adults		
	CTF	1994				

DIABETES MELLITUS

[a]High risk is defined as either (1) obesity (BMI ≥ 27 kg/m^2) + age < 25 years (see BMI Conversion Table in Appendix IV), (2) family history of diabetes in a first-degree relative, or (3) membership in one of the following ethnic groups: black, Hispanic, Native American, Asian American, or Pacific Islander.

[b]High risk is defined as maternal age ≥ 30 years, family history of diabetes, previous macrosomia, malformed or stillborn infants, hypertension, glucosuria, or previous gestational diabetes.

[c]High risk is defined as either (1) age ≥ 45 years; (2) family history of diabetes in parents or siblings; (3) membership in one of the following ethnic groups: black, Hispanic, Native American, Asian American, or Pacific Islander; (4) history of impaired fasting glucose, impaired glucose tolerance, gestational diabetes, or mother with infant birth weight > 9 lb; or (5) comorbid conditions, including hypertension (≥ 140/90 mm Hg) or dyslipidemia (HDL ≤ 35 mg/dL or TGs ≥ 250 mg/dL).

Disease Screening	Organization	Date	Population	Recommendations	Comments	Source
Domestic Violence & Abuse	ACOG	1996	Women	Recommend routine, direct questions about domestic violence.	Controversy exists regarding the overall benefit of mandatory reporting of domestic violence. (JAMA 1995;273:1781)	
	ACOG	1996	Elderly		Some states have mandatory reporting of elder abuse and neglect.	
Hearing Impairment	AAP Joint Committee on Infant Hearing Bright Futures NIH	1999 1995 1994 1993	Normal-risk infants and children	All infants should be screened before 3 months of age with auditory brainstem response or otoacoustic emissions. Perform pure-tone audiometry at 3, 4, 5, 10, 12, 15, and 18 years of age.		Pediatrics 1995;95(1):152 Pediatrics 1999;10(2):527 NIH Consens Statement 1993;11:1
	USPSTF CTF	1996 1994	Normal-risk infants and children	Insufficient evidence to recommend for or against routine screening of neonates Routine screening beyond age 3 years is not recommended.		

Disease Screening	Organization	Date	Population	Recommendations	Comments	Source
				HEARING IMPAIRMENT		
Hearing Impairment (continued)	ASHA	1991	Normal-risk infants and children	Annual pure-tone audiometry for children functioning at a developmental level of age 3 years to grade 3		ASHA Suppl 1991;33:37
	USPSTF Joint Committee on Infant Hearing	1996 1995	High-risk infants and children[a,b]	Infants should be screened no later than 3 months of age. Screen infants and children < 2 years of age with increased risk. Screen every 6 months until 3 years of age if there is risk for delayed-onset hearing loss.		Pediatrics 1995;95(1):152
	AAP ASHA	1995 1990	High-risk children[b]	Children with frequent recurrent otitis media or middle-ear effusion, or both, should have audiology screening and monitoring of communication-skills development.		Pediatrics 1995;95(1):152 ASHA Suppl 1990;32:17
	AGS AAFP USPSTF ACOG CTF	1997 1997 1996 1996 1994	Adults	Question older adults periodically about hearing impairment, counsel about availability of hearing-aid devices, and make referrals for abnormalities when appropriate.		J Am Geriatr Soc 1997;45:344 http://www.aafp.org/ exam/app-d_c.html

HEARING IMPAIRMENT

[a] Increased neonatal risk: family history of hereditary sensorineural hearing loss, intrauterine infection, craniofacial anomalies, birth weight < 1,500 g, hyperbilirubinemia requiring exchange transfusions, ototoxic medications, bacterial meningitis, Apgar scores 0–4 and 0–6, mechanical ventilation lasting > 5 days, and stigmata associated with a syndrome known to include hearing loss.

[b] Increased childhood risk: patient/caregiver concern regarding hearing, speech, language, or developmental delay; bacterial meningitis; head trauma associated with loss of consciousness or skull fracture; stigmata associated with a syndrome known to include hearing loss; ototoxic medications; recurrent or persistent otitis media with effusion; disorders affecting eustachian tube function; neurofibromatosis type 2; and neurodegenerative disorders. Delayed-onset hearing loss: as above for increased childhood risk plus family history of hereditary childhood hearing loss and intrauterine infection.

HEPATITIS B VIRUS						
Disease Screening	Organization	Date	Population	Recommendations	Comments	Source
Hepatitis B Virus Infection, Chronic	AAP and ACOG USPSTF ACP ACIP	1996 1997 1994 1993 1991	Pregnant women	Screen all women with HBsAg[a] at first prenatal visit. Repeat in third trimester if woman is initially HBsAg negative and engages in high-risk behavior.[b]	Screening all pregnant women in the US each year is estimated to detect 22,000 HBsAg-positive mothers, and treatment of their newborns would prevent chronic HBV infection in 6,000 neonates per year. (Pediatr Infect Dis J 1992;11:866)	MMWR 1991;40(RR-13):1 Int J Gynaecol Obstet 1993:40-172
	AAP and ACOG USPSTF ACP ACIP	1996 1997 1994 1993 1991	General population	Routine screening is not recommended.		
	AAP and ACOG USPSTF ACP ACIP	1996 1997 1994 1993 1991	High-risk persons[b]	Insufficient evidence to recommend for or against screening to determine eligibility for vaccination, but recommendations for screening may be made based on cost-effectiveness analyses		

HEPATITIS B VIRUS

[a] Immunoassays for HBsAg have sensitivity and specificity > 98%. (MMWR 1993;42:707)

[b] High risk includes injection drug users, sexual contact with HBV-infected persons or with persons at high risk for HBV infection, multiple sexual partners, and male homosexual activity

HEPATITIS C VIRUS

Disease Screening	Organization	Date	Population	Recommendations	Comments	Source
Hepatitis C Virus Infection, Chronic	CDC AAP	1998 1998	Persons at increased risk[a]	Perform routine counseling, testing, and appropriate follow-up.[b] See figure below.		MMWR 1998;47(RR-19):1 Pediatrics 1998;101(3):481

[a]Increased risk includes injection drug use, receipt of clotting factor concentrates before 1987, chronic hemodialysis, persistently abnormal ALT levels, receipt of blood from a donor who later tested positive for HCV, receipt of blood transfusion or blood components before July 1992, receipt of organ transplant before July 1992, health care workers after needle sticks or mucosal exposures to HCV-positive blood, and children born to HCV-positive women.

[b]Two types of tests are available for laboratory diagnosis of HCV infection: (1) detection of antibody to HCV antigens, and (2) detection and quantification of HCV nucleic acid. See algorithm below.

HCV INFECTION TESTING ALGORITHM FOR ASYMPTOMATIC PERSONS

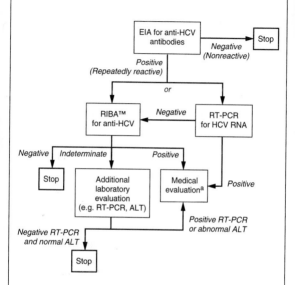

ALT = alanine aminotransferase; anti-HCV = antibody to HCV; EIA = enzyme immunoassay; RIBA™ = recombinant immunoblot assay; RT-PCR = reverse transcriptase polymerase chain reaction

[a]For possible anti-inflammatory and antiviral treatments.

Source: Adapted from MMWR 1998;47(RR-19):1.

HUMAN IMMUNODEFICIENCY VIRUS, (HIV)

Disease Screening	Organization	Date	Population	Recommendations	Comments	Source
Human Immunodeficiency Virus	AAFP	1997	People at increased risk[a]	Counseling and testing for HIV should be offered.	*Initial screening test:* EIA is considered reactive only when a positive result is confirmed in a second test of the original sample. Seroconversion is 95% within 6 months of infection. Specificity is > 99.5%. False-positives with EIA: nonspecific reactions in persons with immunologic disturbances (eg, systemic lupus erythematosus or rheumatoid arthritis), multiple transfusions, recent influenza, or rabies vaccination. Confirmatory testing is necessary using Western blot or indirect immunofluorescence assay. Home tests available[b]	Pediatrics 1993;92:626
	USPSTF	1996				MMWR 1993;42(RR-2):1
	Bright Futures	1994				MMWR 1987;36:509
	GAPS	1994				MMWR 1995;44(RR-7):1
	CTF	1994				Am Intern Med 1994;120:310
	ACP	1994				Pediatrics 1995;95(2):303
	AAP	1993				www.aafp.org/exam/app–d_c.html
	AMA	1993				AMA: HIV Blood Test Counseling.
	CDC	1993				Physician Guidelines. 2nd ed.
	ACOG	1992				AMA, 1993.

HUMAN IMMUNODEFICIENCY VIRUS, (HIV)

Disease Screening	Organization	Date	Population	Recommendations	Comments	Source
Human Immunodeficiency Virus (continued)	AAFP USPSTF ACOG AAP CDC	1997 1996 1996 1995 1995	Pregnant women	Counsel pregnant women about the potential benefit to their infant of early intervention for HIV and offer testing at first prenatal visit. Repeat testing in third trimester for women at high risk of recent exposure to HIV[a]		Pediatrics 1995;95:303 N Engl J Med 1994;331:1173

[a]High risk: seeking treatment for STDs; male homosexual sex after 1975; male partners of people who are HIV-infected, bisexual, or injection drug users; or history of blood transfusion between 1978 and 1985.

[b]The FDA has approved 2 HIV home testing kits and warns about use of HIV home testing kits that have not been FDA approved. Consumers can obtain information about HIV home testing kits by calling the HIV/AIDS Program of the FDA in the Office of Special Health Issues at 301-827-4460. Health care provider follow-up is recommended for positive home HIV test results. (Oncology 1999;13(1):81)

HYPERTENSION, CHILDREN & ADOLESCENTS

Disease Screening	Organization	Date	Population	Recommendations	Comments	Source
Hypertension, Children & Adolescents	USPSTF	1996	Age < 21 years	"During office visits"	Hypertension: BP > 95th percentile 3 different times within 1 month, adjusted for height (J Pediatr 1993;123:871) (see Appendix III) Major reason to screen children is early identification of conditions associated with hypertension (eg. coarctation of aorta, renal artery stenosis, renal parenchymal disease). Treatment: See[a] below.	Pediatrics 1987;79:1 Pediatrics 1996;98:649
	NHLBI	1996	Ages 3–20 years	Annual screening		
	Bright Futures	1994	Ages 3–21 years	Annual screening at ages 3–6, 8, and 10–21 years		
	GAPS	1994	Ages 11–18 years	Annual screening		

HYPERTENSION, ADULTS						
Disease Screening	Organization	Date	Population	Recommendations	Comments	Source
Hypertension, Adults	JNC VI	1997	Age ≥ 18 years	Annual screening If BP < 130/85 mm Hg, then every 2 years If BP 130–139/85–89 mm Hg, then annually If BP 140–159/90–99 mm Hg, then confirm within 2 months	Hypertension: SBP > 140 or DBP > 90 mm Hg Finger monitors are not accurate. (Fam Med 1996;61(50):53) Perform physical exam and routine labs.[b] Pursue secondary causes of hypertension.[c] Treatment: See[de] below.	Arch Intern Med 1997;157:2413
	USPSTF	1996	Age ≥ 21 years	Periodic screening If BP < 140/85 mm Hg, then every 2 years If DBP 85–89 mm Hg, then annually		
	CTF	1994	Age ≥ 21 years	BP screening at any visit		

HYPERTENSION, ELDERLY

Disease Screening	Organization	Date	Population	Recommendations	Comments	Source
Hypertension, Elderly	JNC VI	1997	Age ≥ 60 years	Annual screening	Prevalence: 60–70% of persons > 60 years old Treatment[f] (JNC VI SBP goal < 140 mm Hg)	Hypertension 1995;25:305 N Engl J Med 1993;329:1912

[a]Treatment of primary (essential) hypertension in older children and adolescents is of unproved benefit; majority respond to weight loss and exercise. (Am J Cardiol 1983;52:763, Pediatrics 1978;61:245) The NHLBI recommends pharmacologic treatment of severe hypertension in addition to nonpharmacologic treatment (less than 1% of hypertensive children are classified as severe). (Arch Dis Child 1967;42:34)

[b]Physical exam should include: measurements of height, weight, and waist circumference; fundoscopic exam (retinopathy); carotid auscultation (bruit); jugular venous pulsation; thyroid gland (enlargement); cardiac auscultation (left ventricular heave, S3 or S4, murmurs, clicks); chest auscultation (rales, evidence of chronic obstructive pulmonary disease); abdominal exam (bruits, masses, pulsations); exam of lower extremities (diminished arterial pulsations, bruits, edema); and neurologic exam (focal findings). Routine labs include urinalysis, complete blood count, electrolytes, creatinine, fasting glucose, lipids, and 12-lead electrocardiogram.

[c]Pursue secondary causes of hypertension when evaluation is suggestive (clues in parentheses) of: (1) pheochromocytoma (labile or paroxysmal hypertension accompanied by sweats, headaches, and palpitations); (2) renovascular disease (abdominal bruits), (3) autosomal dominant polycystic kidney disease (abdominal or flank masses), (4) Cushing's syndrome (truncal obesity with purple striae), (5) primary hyperaldosteronism (hypokalemia), (6) hyperparathyroidism (hypercalcemia), (7) renal parenchymal disease (elevated serum creatinine, abnormal urinalysis), (8) poor response to drug therapy, (9) well-controlled hypertension with an abrupt increase in blood pressure, (10) SBP ≥ 180 or DBP ≥ 110 mm Hg, or (11) sudden onset of hypertension.

HYPERTENSION

[d]Treatment includes: (1) lifestyle modifications to affect blood pressure: Lose weight, limit alcohol to < 2 servings/d for men (< 1 serving/d for women), increase aerobic activity (30–45 min/d), reduce sodium intake (< 2.4 g of sodium or 6.0 g NaCl), maintain adequate dietary potassium (fruits and vegetables), and maintain adequate dietary calcium and magnesium. Note that the salt restriction recommendations are particularly applicable to black, elderly, and diabetic patients. (2) Lifestyle modifications to decrease heart disease risk: Reduce saturated fatty acid intake, trans-fatty acids, and dietary cholesterol; stop smoking.

[e]CHS/BHS pharmacologic treatment recommendations for DBP 90–99 mm Hg are dependent upon additional factors of target organ damage or diabetes. Otherwise, risk stratify according to higher pressures within the range, advanced age, male sex, smoking, dyslipidemia, or strong family history of cardiovascular disease. (BMJ 1993;306:983).

[f]Give pharmacy prescription if SBP > 160 mm Hg. Although SBP of 140–160 mm Hg is associated with greater cardiovascular morbidity, there is still no demonstration that pharmacologic therapy improves outcomes.

LEAD POISONING

Disease Screening	Organization	Date	Population	Recommendations	Comments	Source
Lead Poisoning	AAP CDC	1998 1997	Infants and children	Selective screening with blood lead level at 9–12 months, and again at 24 months when levels peak, of infants at high risk[a] Evaluation of blood lead level[b]		Pediatrics 1998; 101:1072 www.cdc.gov/ nceh/programs/ lead/guide/ 1997/ guide97.htm
	AAFP USPSTF	1996	Infants at age 12 months	Selective screening with blood lead level for those infants at high risk[c]		

[a]High risk of lead poisoning if any one of the following conditions exists: (1) Child lives in or regularly visits a house or child care facility built before 1950; (2) child lives in or regularly visits a house or child care facility built before 1978 that is being or has recently been renovated or remodeled (within the last 6 months); or (3) child has a sibling or playmate who has or did have lead poisoning.

[b]Confirm elevated lead levels with venous sample on screening sample from fingerstick: immediately if > 70 µg/mL, within 48 hours if 45–69 µg/ mL, within 1 week if 20–44 µg/mL, and within 1 month if 10–19 µg/mL. See AAP guidelines for further treatment recommendations.

[c]Increased risk of lead poisoning exists for infants who: (1) live in communities in which the prevalence of lead levels requiring intervention is high or undefined, (2) live in or frequently visit a home built before 1950 with dilapidated paint or with recent or ongoing renovation or remodeling, (3) have close contact with a person who has an elevated lead level, (4) live near lead industry or heavy traffic, or (5) live with someone whose job or hobby involves lead exposure or who uses lead-based pottery or takes traditional remedies that contain lead.

OBESITY

Disease Screening	Organization	Date	Population	Recommendations	Comments	Source
Obesity	NHLBI NIDDKD	1998	Age > 18 years	Calculate BMI for all patients.[a]	The NHLBI makes a strong case for promoting weight loss in overweight individuals, particularly those with hypertension, diabetes, cardiovascular disease, and hyperlipidemia.	NHLBI Obesity Guidelines in Adults, 1998.
	USPSTF AAFP AAP Bright Futures GAPS	1996 1994 1994	All age groups	Periodic height and weight measurements		www.aafp.org/exam

[a]BMI is calculated as: weight (kg)/height (m) squared. See Appendix IV for BMI Conversion Table. Overweight is defined as BMI 25–29.9 kg/m^2 and obesity as BMI $\geq$ 30 kg/m^2.

OSTEOPOROSIS

Disease Screening	Organization	Date	Population	Recommendations	Comments	Source
Osteoporosis	NOF	1998	Women	Bone densitometry should not be routine. It should be considered for those at high risk of osteoporosis. [a]		Ann Intern Med 1990;112:516
	AAFP	1997				Endocrine Practice 1996;2:155
	USPSTF	1996				http://www.nof.org
	ACOG	1996				NIH Consens Dev
	AACE	1996				Conf Consens
	CTF	1994				Statement 1984;5:1
	ACP	1990				http://www.aafp.org/ exam/app-d_c.html

[a]High risk: chronic steroid use, repeated fractures, early menopause, blood relative with osteoporosis, or known low bone mass or bone density. Bone densitometry may be useful to guide treatment in selected postmenopausal women.

SCOLIOSIS

Disease Screening	Organization	Date	Population	Recommendations	Comments	Source
Scoliosis	USPSTF CTF	1996 1994	Adolescents	Insufficient evidence to recommend for or against routine screening of asymptomatic adolescents	Positive predictive value of bending test is 42.8% for scolioses of ≥ 5 degrees and 6.4% for ≥ 15 degrees; sensitivity 74%, specificity 78%. (Am J Public Health 1985;75:1377)	
	Bright Futures	1994	Adolescents	Screen during physical exam in adolescents and children ≥ 8 years of age.		
	AAOS	1992	Adolescents	Screen girls twice (ages 10 and 12 years) and boys once (age 13 or 14 years).		www.aaos.org/ wordhtml/papers/ position/ scolios.htm
	Scoliosis Research Society	1986	Adolescents	Perform annual screening of all children ages 10-14 years.		Scoliosis Research Society: Scoliosis: A Handbook for Patients. Scoliosis Research Society, 1986.

SYPHILIS

Disease Screening	Organization	Date	Population	Recommendations	Comments	Source
Syphilis	AAFP	1997	Pregnant women and high-risk persons[a]	Screen all pregnant women with nontreponemal test (eg, RPR or VDRL) at first prenatal visit; repeat in third trimester and at delivery for women at high risk of acquiring infection during pregnancy. Screen high-risk (nonpregnant) persons with routine serologic test (nontreponemal test; eg, RPR or VDRL).	All reactive nontreponemal tests should be confirmed with a more specific treponemal test (eg, FTA–ABS). Perform follow-up serologic tests after treatment to document decline in titers (using the same test used initially). Sensitivity of nontreponemal tests varies with levels of antibodies: 62–76% in early primary syphilis, 100% during secondary syphilis, and 70% in untreated late syphilis. In late syphilis, previously reactive results revert to nonreactive in 25% of patients. Specificity of nontreponemal tests is 75–85% in persons with preexisting diseases or conditions (eg, collagen vascular diseases, injection drug use, advanced malignancy, pregnancy, malaria, tuberculosis, viral and rickettsial diseases) and 100% in persons without preexisting diseases or conditions.	Ann Intern Med 1986;104:368 Pediatrics 1994;94:568 MMWR 1993;42(RR-14):1 www.aafp.org/exam/app-d_c.html
	AAP & ACOG	1997				
	USPSTF	1996				
	GAPS	1994				
	Bright Futures	1994				
	ACP	1986				

[a]High risk includes commercial sex workers, persons who exchange sex for money or drugs, persons with other STDs (including HIV), and sexual contacts of persons with active syphilis.

					THYROID DISEASE		
Disease Screening	Organization	Date	Population	Recommendations	Comments		Source
Thyroid Disease	USPSTF	1996	Children and adults	Routine screening is not recommended.			
	ATA	1995	Any age group	Selective screening for high-risk patients[a]			JAMA 1995;273:808
	USPSTF	1996	Elderly	Insufficient evidence to recommend for or against screening	Clinicians should remain alert for subtle or nonspecific symptoms of hypothyroidism and maintain a low threshold for diagnostic evaluation using serum TSH. Controversy exists regarding Rx benefit for patients with subclinical hypothyroidism (elevated TSH; normal free thyroxine).		J Gen Intern Med 1996;11:744 Ann Intern Med 1984;101:18
	ATA	1995	Women age > 60 years	Screen once with serum TSH.	The ATA states that therapy for subclinical hypothyroidism is especially advisable for patients with thyroid autoantibodies because there is a high frequency of progression to overt hypothyroidism in this subgroup.		JAMA 1995;273:808
	ACP	1991	Women age > 50 years	Perform selective screening for women with 1 or more general symptoms such as fatigue, weight gain, or depression.			Common Screening Tests. ACP; 1991.

THYROID DISEASE

[a]Increased risk of hypothyroidism among patients with autoimmune diseases, unexplained depression, cognitive dysfunction, or hypercholesterolemia.

TUBERCULOSIS

Disease Screening	Organization	Date	Population	Recommendations	Comments	Source
Tuberculosis	AAFP	1997	Persons at increased risk of developing TB[a]	Screening by tuberculin skin test is recommended. Frequency of testing should be based on likelihood of further exposure to TB and level of confidence in the accuracy of the results. bc	Persons with positive PPD test should receive chest x-ray and clinical evaluation for TB. If no evidence of active infection, provide INH prophylaxis if appropriate.	Am Rev Respir Dis 1992;146:1623
	USPSTF	1996				Pediatrics 1994;93:131
	AAP	1996				Pediatrics 1996;97:282
	CTF	1994				MMWR 1995;44(RR-11):19
	Bright Futures	1994				www.aafp.org/exam/app-d_c.html
	GAPS	1994				
	ATS	1992				

[a]Increased risk: persons infected with HIV, close contacts of persons with known or suspected TB (including health care workers), persons with medical risk factors associated with reactivation of TB (eg, silicosis, diabetes mellitus, prolonged corticosteroid therapy, end-stage renal disease, immunosuppressive therapy), immigrants from countries with high TB prevalence (eg, most countries in Africa, Asia, and Latin America), medically underserved and low-income populations, alcoholics, injection drug users, persons with abnormal chest x-rays compatible with past TB, and residents of long-term care facilities (eg, correctional institutions, mental institutions, nursing homes).

[b]Periodic (eg, ages 1, 4-6, and 6-11 years) tuberculin skin testing is recommended for children who live in high-prevalence regions or whose history for risk factors is incomplete or unreliable.

[c]Test: Give intradermal injection of 5 U of tuberculin PPD and examine 48-72 hours later. Criteria for positive skin test (diameter of induration): ≥ 15 mm for low risk; ≥ 10 mm for high risk (including children < 4 years of age); ≥ 5 mm for very high risk (HIV, abnormal chest radiograph, recent contact with infected persons). If negative, consider 2-step testing to differentiate between booster effect and new conversion. Perform second test within 1-3 weeks. False-negative results occur in 5-10%, especially early in infection, with anergy, with concurrent severe illness, in newborns and infants < 3 months old, and with improper technique. Prior BCG vaccination is not considered a valid basis for dismissing positive results.

VISUAL IMPAIRMENT & GLAUCOMA

Disease Screening	Organization	Date	Population	Recommendations	Comments	Source
Visual Impairment & Glaucoma	AAP Bright Futures AOA AAO	1996 1994 1994 1991	Infants and children	Eye and vision screening is recommended between birth and 2 months, at age 6 months, ages 3–5 years, and ages 5–6 years. AOA recommends continuing comprehensive eye and vision exams every 2 years thereafter.		Pediatrics 1996;98:153 www.aoanet.org/ia-need-exam.html www.eyenet.org
	AAFP USPSTF	1997 1996	Children	Vision screening for amblyopia and strabismus for all children once before entering school, preferably between ages 3 and 4 years Insufficient evidence to recommend for or against routine screening for decreased visual acuity among asymptomatic schoolchildren		www.aafp.org/exam/app-d_c.html
	CTF	1994	Children	Eye and vision screening is recommended during periodic health exams.		

VISUAL IMPAIRMENT & GLAUCOMA

Disease Screening	Organization	Date	Population	Recommendations	Comments	Source
Visual Impairment & Glaucoma (continued)	AAFP USPSTF CTF	1997 1996 1994	Adults	Insufficient evidence to recommend for or against routine eye and vision screening among asymptomatic nonelderly adults		www.aafp.org/exam/app-d_c.html
	AOA	1994	Adults	Comprehensive eye and vision exam every 2–3 years at ages 19–40 years, every 2 years at ages 41–60 years, and every 1 year at age ≥ 61 years	Insufficient evidence to recommend for or against routine ophthalmoscopy or screening for elevated intraocular pressure or glaucoma by primary care physicians	www.aoanet.org/ia-need-exam.html
	AAO	1992	Adults	Comprehensive eye and vision exam every 3–5 years in blacks ages 20–39 years, and, regardless of race, every 2–4 years at ages 40–64 years and every 1–2 years beginning at age 65 years		www.eyenet.org
	AAFP AGS USPSTF CTF	1997 1997 1996 1994	Elderly	Perform routine eye and vision screening. Optimal frequency is not known.		J Am Geriatr Soc 1997;45:344 http://www.aafp.org/exam/app-d_c.html

2

Disease Prevention

BACILLE CALMETTE-GUÉRIN

Immunization	Organization	Date	Population	Recommendations	Comments	Source
Bacille Calmette-Guérin	USPSTF CDC ACIP ATS	1996 1996 1996 1992	Adults[a]	Vaccination with BCG is not recommended for adults in the United States.		Am Rev Respir Dis 1992;146:1623 MMWR 1996;45(RR-4):1018

[a] Consider BCG for health care workers who work in settings in which: (1) A high percentage of TB patients are infected with *M. tuberculosis* resistant to both INH and rifampin; (2) transmission of such drug-resistant strains is likely; and (3) comprehensive infection control precautions have been implemented and have not been successful. Also use BCG for tuberculin-negative infants and children who cannot be placed on INH and who have continuous exposure to persons with active disease and those belonging to groups with a rate of new infections greater than 1% per year and for whom the usual surveillance and treatment programs may not be operationally feasible.

	DIPHTHERIA-TETANUS-PERTUSSIS				
Immunization	Organization	Date	Population	Recommendations	Comments	Source
Diphtheria-Tetanus-Pertussis	ACIP AAFP AAP ACPM	1999 1999 1999 1997	Infants and children	Same schedule as recommended by USPSTF (see Appendix V), but DTaP is the preferred vaccine for all doses in the vaccination series, including completion of the series in children who have received 1 or more doses of DTP. Fourth dose may be given as early as 12 months, provided 6 months have elapsed since the third dose.	DTaP = diphtheria and tetanus toxoids and acellular pertussis vaccine, which has fewer side effects.	MMWR 1999;48:12 Am J Prev Med 1997;13:74 www.aafp.org/exam/app-d_c.html Pediatrics 1997;99(2):282 Pediatrics 1993;91(6):121 MMWR 1997;46(RR-7):1 Am J Prev Med 1997;13(23):74
	USPSTF	1996	Infants and children	Administer DTP vaccine at ages 2, 4, and 6 months; DTP at 12–18 months or DTaP at 15–18 months; and DTP or DTaP between ages 4 and 6 years. Administer Td booster at ages 11–12 years (or 14–16 years).		

DIPHTHERIA-TETANUS-PERTUSSIS						
Immunization	**Organization**	**Date**	**Population**	**Recommendations**	**Comments**	**Source**
Diphtheria-Tetanus-Pertussis (continued)	ACIP AAFP AGS ACOG ACP CTF	1999 1999 1997 1996 1994 1994	Adults	Administer Td booster vaccination every 10 years or single booster at age 50 or 65 years.	If nonimmunized person is age ≥ 7 years, administer 3 doses of Td. Give the second dose 4–8 weeks after the first, and administer the third dose 6–12 months after the second dose.	www.aafp.org/exam/app-d_c.html ACOG: Guidelines for Women's Health Care. ACOG, 1996. ACP: Guide for Adult Immunization, 3rd ed. ACP, 1994. MMWR 1999:48:12 MMWR 1994;43(RR-1):1 J Am Geriatr Soc 1997;45:344
	USPSTF	1996	Adults	All adults should receive a periodic Td booster (optimal interval not established, but standard regimen is every 10 years).		

	HAEMOPHILUS INFLUENZAE TYPE B				HEPATITIS A VIRUS	
Immunization	Organization	Date	Population	Recommendations	Comments	Source
Haemophilus influenzae Type B	ACIP AAFP AAP ACPM CTF	1999 1999 1999 1997 1994	Infants and children	Conjugate vaccine at 2, 4, and 6 months, with a booster dose at 12–15 months. If PRP-OMP is used, a dose at 6 months is not required. CTF recommends booster dose given at 18 months.	Hib vaccination has high efficacy (> 90%) for preventing Hib invasive disease. Since vaccine introduction, there has been a significant decline in the incidence of invasive *H. influenzae* disease. (Clinician's Handbook of Preventive Services, 2nd ed. International Medical Publishers, 1998)	MMWR 1999;48:12 Am J Prev Med 1997;13(23):74
Hepatitis A Virus	AAFP AAP USPSTF ACP	1997 1996 1996 1994	Age ≥ 2 years	Immunize high-risk individuals.[a,b]	If patient requires immediate protection against hepatitis A, administer immune globulin simultaneously with the first vaccine dose.	www.aafp.org/exam/app−1_c.html Pediatrics 1996;98(6):1207 ACP: Guide for Adult Immunization, 3rd ed. ACP, 1994.

[a]High risk: persons living in, traveling to, or working in areas where the disease is endemic and periodic outbreaks occur; institutionalized persons; men who have sex with men; injection drug users; military personnel; and certain hospital and laboratory workers. (See CDC traveler's web site at http:// www.cdc.gov/travel/.)

[b]Schedule: For age < 18 years, 3 doses, with second and third doses given 1 and 6–12 months after the first dose; for age ≥ 18 years, 2 doses, with second dose at 6–12 months.

Immunization	Organization	Date	Population	Recommendations	Comments	Source
HEPATITIS B VIRUS						
Hepatitis B Virus	ACIP AAFP AAP ACPM USPSTF	1999 1999 1999 1997 1996	Infants, children, and adolescents	Immunize all infants, and all children and adolescents not previously immunized.[a][b]		MMWR 1999;48:12 Am J Prev Med 1997;13(23):74 Pediatrics 1997;99(3):479 MMWR 1991;40(RR-13):1
	USPSTF	1996	Young adults High-risk adults[c]	Immunize all young adults not previously vaccinated.[d] Immunize high-risk groups.[d]	Consider testing antibody response in individuals at very high risk of hepatitis B who are likely to have inadequate antibody response (ie, chronic renal dialysis patients, injection drug users, those with HIV infection).	

HEPATITIS B VIRUS

[a]Schedule: Immunize at ages 0–2 months, then 1–2 months after the first dose, then at ages 6–18 months. After infancy, give first dose, followed by second and third doses at 1 and 6 months.

[b]Infants of HBsAg-negative mothers: Second dose should be at least 1 month after the first. Third dose should be at least 4 months after the first dose and at least 2 months after the second dose, but not before age 6 months. Infants of HBsAg-positive mothers: Give hepatitis B vaccine and hepatitis B immune globulin within 12 hours of birth, second dose at ages 1–2 months, and third dose at age 6 months. Infants for whom maternal HBsAg status is unknown: Give hepatitis B vaccine within 12 hours of birth and determine maternal HBsAg status: If positive, provide hepatitis B immune globulin as soon as possible (no later than age 1 week).

[c]High risk: men who have had sex with men, injection drug users and their sexual partners, history of sexual activity with multiple partners or history of another STD, international travelers to countries where HBV is of high or intermediate endemicity, recipients of certain blood products (including hemodialysis patients), and persons in health-related jobs with frequent exposure to blood or blood products.

[d]Recommended regimen: initial vaccine, then repeat at 1 and 6 months.

Immunization	Organization	Date	Population	Recommendations	Comments	Source
INFLUENZA						
Influenza	AAFP AGS ACIP USPSTF ACP CTF	1997 1997 1997 1996 1994 1994	Ages 6 months to 64 years	Administer annually to high-risk persons.[a]	Influenza vaccination has also been shown to decrease work loss days in otherwise healthy, nonelderly adults. (N Engl J Med 1995;333:889)	www.aafp.org/exam/app-d_c.html MMWR 1997;46(RR-9):1 ACP: Guide for Adult Immunization, 3rd ed. ACP, 1994.
	ACOG	1996	Women age ≥ 60 years	Administer annually.		
	AAFP AGS ACIP USPSTF ACP CTF	1997 1997 1997 1996 1994 1994	Age ≥ 65 years	Administer annually.		J Am Geriatr Soc 1997;45:344 www.aafp.org/exam/app-d_c.html MMWR 1997;46(RR-9):1 ACP: Guide for Adult Immunization, 3rd ed. ACP, 1994.
	ACP	1994	Health care providers and household members of high-risk persons[a]	Administer annually.		ACP: Guide for Adult Immunization, 3rd ed. ACP, 1994.

[a]High risk: residents of chronic care facilities and persons with chronic cardiopulmonary disorders, metabolic diseases (including diabetes mellitus), hemoglobinopathies, immunosuppression, or renal dysfunction.

MEASLES-MUMPS-RUBELLA

Immunization	Organization	Date	Population	Recommendations	Comments	Source
Measles-Mumps-Rubella	ACIP	1999	Children	Administer at ages 12–15 months and again at 4–6 years of age; 11–12 years is an acceptable alternative for second dose.	Children age > 6 years who have not yet received 2 doses should be vaccinated, with the goal that all children will have had 2 doses of MMR vaccine by ages 11–12.	MMWR 1999;48:12
	AAFP	1999				Am J Prev Med 1997;13:74
	AAP	1999				Clinician's Handbook of Preventive Services, 2nd ed. International Medical Publishing, 1998.
	ACPM	1997				
	USPSTF	1996				Pediatrics 1998;101(1):129
						www.aafp.org/exam/ app–d_c.html
						Am J Prev Med 1997;13(23):74
	AAFP	1997	Women of childbearing age	Obtain history of vaccination, or offer serology, or offer vaccination (for rubella).	Do not administer rubella vaccine to pregnant women. Women receiving vaccine should not become pregnant for 3 months after vaccination.	www.aafp.org/exam/ app–d_c.html
	USPSTF	1996				ACP: Guide for Adult Immunization, 3rd ed. ACP, 1994.
	ACOG	1996				
	ACP	1994				MMWR 1994;43(RR-1):1
	CTF	1994				
	ACIP	1994				
	ACP	1994	Health care workers	ACP recommends documentation of serologic immunity or vaccination of all health care workers.		ACP: Guide for Adult Immunization, 3rd ed. ACP, 1994.

POLIOMYELITIS VIRUS

Immunization	Organization	Date	Population	Recommendations	Comments	Source
Poliomyelitis Virus	ACIP AAFP AAP ACPM	1999 1999 1999 1997	Infants and children	Give IPV at ages 2 months and 4 months, OPV at 6–18 months and 4-6 years.[a], [b]	The WHO has established a target of the end of the year 2000 for global eradication of poliomyelitis.	MMWR 1999;48:12 Pediatrics 1999;103(1):171 Am J Prev Med 1997;13(23):74
	ACPM USPSTF	1997 1996	Infants and children	Give OPV at ages 2 months, 4 months, 6–18 months, and 4-6 years.		Am J Prev Med 1997;13(23):74

[a] IPV is recommended for immunocompromised persons and their household contacts.
[b] To eliminate the risk of vaccine-associated paralytic polio (VAPP), an all-IPV schedule is recommended as of January 2000 for routine childhood polio vaccination in the U.S. (see Appendix V).

STREPTOCOCCUS PNEUMONIAE

Immunization	Organization	Date	Population	Recommendations	Comments	Source
Streptococcus pneumoniae	AAFP	1997	Ages 2–64 years	Immunize high-risk persons.[a]	Routine revaccination is not recommended but may be appropriate and is safe in individuals at highest risk for morbidity and mortality from pneumococcal disease who were vaccinated > 5 years previously or if age was < 65 years at the time of primary vaccination. (MMWR 1997;46(RR-8):1)	www.aafp.org/exam/ app-d_c.html ACP: Guide for Adult Immunization, 3rd ed. ACP, 1994. MMWR 1997;46(RR-8):1
	ACIP	1997				
	USPSTF	1996				
	ACOG	1996				
	ACP	1994				
	CTF	1994	Age ≥ 55 years	Insufficient evidence to recommend for or against immunization for immunocompetent individuals age ≥ 55 years living independently. Good evidence to recommend for immunocompetent individuals age ≥ 55 years living in institutions and patients with history of sickle cell disease or history of splenectomy.		

STREPTOCOCCUS PNEUMONIAE

Immunization	Organization	Date	Population	Recommendations	Comments	Source
***Streptococcus pneumoniae* (continued)**	AGS AAFP ACIP USPSTF ACOG ACP	1997 1997 1997 1996 1996 1994	Age ≥ 65 years	Recommended for all individuals age ≥ 65 years.		J Am Geriatr Soc 1997;45:344 www.aafp.org/exam/app-d_c.html MMWR 1997;46(RR-8):1 ACP: Guide for Adult Immunization, 3rd ed. ACP, 1994.

[a]Increased risk: institutionalized persons age ≥ 50 years, chronic cardiac or pulmonary disease, diabetes mellitus, anatomic asplenia, special environments with increased risk of pneumococcal disease (eg, certain Native American and Alaska Native populations), alcoholism, cirrhosis, chronic renal failure, nephrotic syndrome, sickle cell disease, multiple myeloma, metastatic or hematologic malignancy, and acquired or congenital immunodeficiency.

VARICELLA VIRUS

Immunization	Organization	Date	Population	Recommendations	Comments	Source
Varicella Virus	ACIP AAFP AAP ACPM USPSTF	1999 1999 1999 1997 1996	All[a]	Give 1 dose at any visit on or after the first birthday for susceptible children (lacking reliable history or never vaccinated).	Consider offering serologic testing to adolescents and adults without reliable history of infection or immunization.	MMWR 1999;48:12 Am J Prev Med 1997;13(23):74 Pediatrics 1995;95(5):791 MMWR 1996;45(RR-11):1
	ACIP AAFP AAP ACPM USPSTF	1999 1999 1999 1997 1996	Persons age ≥ 13 years with unknown history of childhood chickenpox	Give 2 doses at least 4 weeks apart.[b]		MMWR 1999;48:12 Am J Prev Med 1997;13(23):74 Pediatrics 1995;95(5):791 MMWR 1996;45(RR-11):1

[a]Varicella vaccine should not be given routinely to immunocompromised individuals. The presence of an immunodeficient household contact does not contraindicate vaccine use in other household members.

[b]Loss of immunity to varicella may wane after vaccination, but no evidence of loss of immunity has been noted in 6–10 years of follow-up while wild-type varicella continues to circulate. As a result of widespread but not universal use of vaccine, an increased rate of clinical cases of varicella could occur in adults who were not vaccinated as children.

BREAST CANCER							
Disease	Organization	Date	Population	Recommendations	Comments	Source
Breast Cancer	NCI	1999	Women	Avoid unnecessary breast irradiation. Little evidence to support or quantify potential beneficial effect of genetic screening (BRCA1/BRCA2) Low-fat diet and exercise may decrease risk. Less than 50% of all breast cancer cases are attributable to well-established risk factors; many risk factors are not modifiable. Tamoxifen: Need further data to estimate benefit.		cancernet.nci.nih. gov/clinpdq/ screening

BREAST CANCER

Disease	Organization	Date	Population	Recommendations	Comments	Source
Breast Cancer (continued)	ASCO	1998	Women at high risk[a]	For women with a 5-year projected risk of breast cancer of ≥ 1.66%, tamoxifen (at 20 mg/d for up to 5 years) may be offered to reduce their risk. Tamoxifen use should be discussed as part of an informed decision-making process, with careful consideration of risks and benefits. Premature to recommend raloxifene use to lower the risk of developing breast cancer outside of a clinical trial setting[b]	Women being considered for tamoxifen therapy should be evaluated by health care providers familiar with evaluation of individual breast cancer risk and the risks and benefits of tamoxifen use. Currently insufficient evidence to determine whether tamoxifen provides overall health benefit or increased breast cancer-specific or overall survival.	www.asco.org J Clin Oncol 1999;17(6):1939

[a] Predicted risk of breast cancer calculated by using the Gail model, which considers age, number of first-degree relatives with breast cancer, number of previous breast biopsies, age at first live birth, and age at menarche. (J Natl Cancer Inst 1989;81:1879)

[b] Among postmenopausal women with osteoporosis, the risk of invasive breast cancer was decreased by 75% during 3 years of treatment with raloxifene. (JAMA 1999;281(23):2189) The Study of Tamoxifen and Raloxifene (STAR) began recruiting volunteers in May 1999. This study will compare tamoxifen and raloxifene for their effects on reduction of breast cancer development in postmenopausal women. Information is available from http://cancertrials.nci.nih.gov/ or from the National Cancer Institute's Cancer Information Service (1-800-422-6237).

ENDOCARDITIS

Disease	Organization	Date	Population	Recommendations	Comments	Source
Endocarditis	AHA	1997	High-risk persons[a] Moderate-risk persons[b]	Give antibiotic prophylaxis[c] before bacteremia-producing procedures.[d,e]		JAMA 1997;277:1794

[a]Patients at high risk for endocarditis include those with prosthetic heart valves (including bioprosthetic and homograft valves), previous bacterial endocarditis, complex cyanotic congenital heart disease (including single ventricle states, transposition of the great arteries, tetralogy of Fallot), and surgically constructed systemic pulmonary shunts or conduits.

[b]Patients at moderate risk for endocarditis include those with most other congenital heart disease (excluding isolated secundum atrial septal defect and surgically repaired atrial septal defect, ventricular septal defect, or patent ductus arteriosus without residua beyond 6 months), acquired valvular dysfunction (eg, rheumatic heart disease), hypertrophic cardiomyopathy, and mitral valve prolapse with valvar regurgitation or thickened leaflets.

[c]Standard prophylaxis regimen for dental, oral, respiratory tract, or esophageal procedures: amoxicillin (adults 2.0 g; children 50 mg/kg orally 1 hour before procedure). If unable to take oral medications, give ampicillin (adults 2.0 g; children 50 mg/kg IM or IV within 30 minutes of procedure). If penicillin-allergic, give clindamycin (adults 600 mg; children 20 mg/kg orally 1 hour before procedure) or cephalexin or cefadroxil (adults 2.0 g; children 50 mg/kg orally 1 hour before procedure) or azithromycin or clarithromycin (adults 500 mg; children 15 mg/kg orally 1 hour before procedure). If penicillin-allergic and unable to take oral medications, give clindamycin (adults 600 mg; children 20 mg/kg IV within 30 minutes before procedure) or cefazolin (adults 1 g; children 25 mg/kg IM or IV within 30 minutes of procedure). See reference for recommended antibiotic regimens for other procedures. (JAMA 1997;277:1794)

[d]Bacteremia-producing procedures include: (1) dental and oral procedures including dental extractions, periodontal procedures, dental implant placement and reimplantation of avulsed teeth, endodontic (root canal) instrumentation, subgingival placement of antibiotic fibers or strips, initial placement of orthodontic bands but not brackets, intraligamentary local anesthetic injections, and prophylactic cleaning of teeth or implants where bleeding is anticipated; (2) respiratory tract procedures including tonsillectomy and adenoidectomy, surgical operations involving the respiratory mucosa, and bronchoscopy with a rigid bronchoscope; and (3) genitourinary tract procedures including prostatic surgery, cystoscopy, and urethral dilation.

[e]Prophylaxis for high-risk but not moderate-risk patients is recommended for patients undergoing gastrointestinal tract procedures including sclerotherapy, esophageal stricture dilation, ERCP with biliary obstruction, biliary tract surgery, and surgical operations involving the intestinal mucosa.

MYOCARDIAL INFARCTION

Disease	Organization	Date	Population	Recommendations	Comments	Source
Myocardial Infarction	AHA	1997	All	Diet modifications include AHA step I diet ($\leq$ 30% fat, < 10% saturated fat, < 300 mg/d cholesterol). Exercise regularly: 3–4 times per week for 30 minutes. Control weight: achieve and maintain BMI at 21–25 kg/m^2 (see Appendix IV). Strongly encourage smoking cessation.		Circulation 1997;95:2330
	AHA	1997	Hyperlipidemia	Primary prevention of MI includes diet and HMG-CoA reductase inhibitors in patients without a history of CHD and < 2 CHD risk factors[a] (goal LDL < 160 mg/dL) or $\geq$ 2 CHD risk factors (goal LDL < 130 mg/dL). For screening recommendations, see Appendix VII for complete evaluation and treatment algorithms.	RCT's have demonstrated the CHD and mortality benefit and safety of treatment of patients with hypercholesterolemia (pravastatin 40 mg/d) (N Engl J Med 1995;333:1301) and the CHD benefit of treatment of average cholesterol and LDL levels (but low HDL) (lovastatin 20–40 mg/d). (JAMA 1998;279:1615)	Circulation 1997;95:2330

MYOCARDIAL INFARCTION

Disease	Organization	Date	Population	Recommendations	Comments	Source
Myocardial Infarction (continued)	AHA	1997	Hypertension	BP goal: ≤ 140/90 mm Hg. See Appendix VII for JNC VI treatment algorithms.	Since JNC VI (1997), RCTs now support all 4 major drug classes as first-line therapy for hypertension. Meta-analysis suggests that beta-blockers should not be first-line therapy for uncomplicated hypertension in persons age > 60 years. (JAMA 1998;279:1903)	Arch Intern Med 1997;157:2413
	AHA	1997	Diabetes	Treat diabetes to achieve HbA$_{1c}$ < 1 unit above normal (see Appendix VII for diabetes treatment algorithm).	ACE inhibitors should be first choice for diabetics with hypertension. (N Engl J Med 1998;338:645, BMJ 1998;317:703, Diabetes Care 1998;21:597) Studies are supporting more aggressive BP control in this population (eg, < 130/80 mm Hg). (Lancet 1998;351:1755)	Arch Intern Med 1997;157:2413

[a]CHD risk factors include age (men > 44 years, women > 54 years or postmenopausal), hypertension, diabetes, smoking, HDL < 35 mg/dL, and family history of CHD in first-degree relatives (male relatives < 55 years, female relatives < 65 years). If HDL ≥ 60 mg/dL, subtract 1 risk factor from number of positive risk factors.

OSTEOPOROSIS

Disease	Organization	Date	Population	Recommendations	Comments	Source
Osteoporosis	NOF	1998	Women	Counsel all women about potential benefits and risks of hormone prophylaxis (HRT) and about fracture risk reduction (dietary calcium, vitamin D, weight-bearing exercise, smoking cessation).[a]	A recent study suggests that an estrogen-progestin regimen (increased RR = 0.12 per year of treatment) increases breast cancer risk beyond that associated with estrogen alone (increased RR = 0.03 per year of treatment) among women with BMI ≤ 24.4 Kg/m^2 (JAMA 2000; 283:485)	NIH Consens Statement 1994;12:1
	AAFP	1997				NIH Consens Dev Conf Consens Statement 1984;5:1
	USPSTF	1996				Endocrine Practice 1996;2:155
	ACOG	1996				www.nof.org
	AACE	1996				www.aafp.org/exam/app-d_c.html
	CTF	1994				
	ACP	1990				

[a]Recommended HRT: 0.625 mg conjugated estrogen or equivalent once daily; for women with a uterus, add 2.5 mg MPA or equivalent daily or 5–10 mg MPA daily for 10–14 days each month to decrease the risk of endometrial cancer. For women unable to tolerate estrogen who are at high risk for fracture, consider alendronate. Recommended calcium: teens to 20s, 1200 mg/d; 20s to menopause, 1000 mg/d; postmenopause, 1500 mg/d. (NIH Consens Statement 1994;12:1)

STROKE

Disease	Organization	Date	Population	Recommendations	Comments	Source
Stroke	JNC VI	1997	Hypertension	See page 44 for screening and diagnosis recommendations. See Appendix VII for JNC VI hypertension management algorithm.		Arch Intern Med 1997;157:2413
	AHA	1996	Atrial fibrillation	Guideline emphasizes: (1) restoration and maintenance of sinus rhythm, (2) ventricular rate control, and (3) prevention of thromboembolism. See Appendix VII for atrial fibrillation management algorithm.		Circulation 1996; 93;1262
	ACCP	1995	Atrial fibrillation	Give anticoagulation with warfarin; target prothrombin time INR = 2.0–3.0. All patients with ≥ 1 risk factor for stroke[a]. Give warfarin as above. Age < 65 years and no risk factors: Give no treatment or aspirin. Age ≥ 65 years and no risk factors: Give aspirin or oral anticoagulants.		Chest 1995; 108:Suppl.
	ACP	1994	Atrial fibrillation	Similar to ACCP, except uses age 60 years as cutoff for no risk factors		Ann Intern Med 1994; 121:54

Disease	Organization	Date	Population	Recommendations	Comments	Source
Stroke **(Continued)**	AHA CNS USPSTF CTF SVS	1998 1997 1996 1994 1992	CAS	See page 24 for screening and treatment guidelines. Clear consensus exists on efficacy of treatment for symptomatic CAS; treatment of asymptomatic CAS is controversial.		www.american heart.org CMAJ 1997; 157:653 J Vasc Surg 1992; 15:469

[a]Risk factors for subsequent stroke in patients with atrial fibrillation include previous transient ischemic attack or stroke, hypertension, diabetes, thyrotoxicosis, mitral stenosis, or other forms of heart disease.

3
Disease Management

HEDIS© Conditions,
Performance Measures, and
Management Strategies

HEDIS© CONDITIONS AND PERFORMANCE MEASURES

Condition	HEDIS Performance Measure	Management Strategy	Source
Asthma	% receiving anti-inflammatory Rx	See NHLBI evaluation and treatment algorithms in Appendix VII.	www.nhlbi.gov/ling/asthma/prof/practgde.htm
Cardiovascular Disease, Atrial Fibrillation	% with therapeutic INR (2.0–3.0)	See AHA evaluation and treatment algorithms in Appendix VII.	Circulation 1996;93:1262
Cardiovascular Disease, Congestive Heart Failure	% receiving ACE inhibitor	AHA recommends ACE inhibitor therapy in all patients with reduced LV ejection fraction, unless contraindicated.	Circulation 1995;92:2764
Cardiovascular Disease, Hypertension	% with SBP < 140 mm Hg % with DBP < 90 mm Hg	See JNV VI treatment algorithm in Appendix VII.	Arch Intern Med 1997;157:2413
Cardiovascular Disease, Post-Myocardial Infarction	% receiving beta-blocker % LDL checked % LDL < 130 mg/dL	See AHA evaluation and treatment algorithms for hyperlipidemia in Appendix VII.	Circulation 1997;95:2330

Depression	% with ≥ 3 follow-up visits during initial 12-week Rx phase % with adequate acute-phase Rx trial % completing a period of continuation Rx (6 months)	See AHCPR treatment algorithm in Appendix VII. An update from the AHCPR Depression Guideline Panel, using data published since the guideline was developed, concludes: (1) Total treatment costs per depressive episode are similar for patients treated with selective serotonin reuptake inhibitors and tricyclic antidepressants; and (2) clinical and functional outcomes are improved at a cost of $750–1500 per enhanced treatment episode (ie, standard care vs guideline care). Arch Gen Psychiatry 1998;55:1121	
Diabetes Mellitus	% with HbA$_{1c}$ checked at least once in past year[a] % with HbA$_{1c}$ > 9.5% % with lipid profile performed in past 2 years % with LDL < 130 mg/dL in past 2 years % with dilated eye exam in past 1–2 years[b] % with nephropathy screen in past 1–2 years[c] % with BP < 140/90 mm Hg	See ADA treatment recommendations in Appendix VII.	www.diabetes.org/dqip.asp
Women's Health, Breast Cancer Screening	% women receiving mammography	See pages 5 to 7 for various organizational recommendations regarding mammography screening.	
Women's Health, Cervical Cancer screening and Prevention	% women receiving Pap smear	See Pap smear evaluation and management strategies in Appendix VII.	

HEDIS© CONDITIONS AND PERFORMANCE MEASURES

Condition	HEDIS Performance Measure	Management Strategy	Source
Women's Health, Osteoporosis Prevention	% postmenopausal women counseled regarding HRT	See HRT evaluation and management strategies in Appendix VII.	

[a]Optimal HbA$_{1c}$ testing for many patients may require more frequent testing (eg. 3–4 times per year).

[b]Eye exam every 2 years is appropriate if patient is not taking insulin, has a recent HbA$_{1c}$ < 8.0%, and had no retinopathy on previous year's exam.

[c]Nephropathy screen every 2 years is appropriate if patient is not taking insulin, has a recent HbA$_{1c}$ < 8.0%, and had no albuminuria on previous year's exam. Macroalbuminuria screen using dipstick is acceptable if positive; if negative, then ADA recommends proceeding with 24-hour urine protein or microalbumin to creatinine ratio in a random urine collection.

4
Appendices

SCREENING INSTRUMENTS: ALCOHOL ABUSE

SENSITIVITY AND SPECIFICITY OF SCREENING TESTS FOR PROBLEM DRINKING

Instrument Name	Screening Questions/Scoring	Threshold Score	Sensitivity/Specificity (%)	Source
CAGE[a]	See table below	≥1 ≥2 ≥3	77/58 53/81 29/92	Am J Psychiatr 1974;131:1121 J Gen Intern Med 1998;13:379
AUDIT	See table below	≥4 ≥5 ≥6	87/70 77/84 66/90	BMJ 1997;314:420 J Gen Intern Med 1998;13:379

[a]The CAGE may be less applicable to binge drinkers (eg, college students), the elderly, and minority populations.

SCREENING INSTRUMENTS: ALCOHOL ABUSE

SCREENING PROCEDURES FOR PROBLEM DRINKING

1. CAGE screening test[a]

   Have you ever felt the need to **Cut down on drinking?**

   Have you ever felt **Annoyed by criticism of your drinking?**

   Have you ever felt **Guilty about your drinking?**

   Have you ever taken a morning **Eye opener?**

   INTERPRETATION: Two "yes" answers are considered a positive screen. One "yes" answer should arouse a suspicion of alcohol abuse.

2. The alcohol use disorder identification test (AUDIT).[b] (Scores for response categories are given in parentheses. Scores range from 0 to 40, with a cutoff score of ≥ 5 indicating hazardous drinking, harmful drinking, or alcohol dependence.)

   1 How often do you have a drink containing alcohol?

   (0) Never (1) Monthly or less (2) Two to four times a month (3) Two or three times a week (4) Four or more times a week

   2 How many drinks containing alcohol do you have on a typical day when you are drinking?

   (0) 1 or 2 (1) 3 or 4 (2) 5 or 6 (3) 7 to 9 (4) 10 or more

   3 How often do you have six or more drinks on one occasion?

   (0) Never (1) Less than monthly (2) Monthly (3) Weekly (4) Daily or almost daily

   4 How often during the past year have you found that you were not able to stop drinking once you had started?

   (0) Never (1) Less than monthly (2) Monthly (3) Weekly (4) Daily or almost daily

   5 How often during the past year have you failed to do what was normally expected of you because of drinking?

   (0) Never (1) Less than monthly (2) Monthly (3) Weekly (4) Daily or almost daily

continued on next page

SCREENING INSTRUMENTS: ALCOHOL ABUSE

SCREENING PROCEDURES FOR PROBLEM DRINKING (CONTINUED)

6 How often during the past year have you needed a first drink in the morning to get yourself going after a heavy drinking session?

(0) Never   (1) Less than monthly   (2) Monthly   (3) Weekly   (4) Daily or almost daily

7 How often during the past year have you had a feeling of guilt or remorse after drinking?

(0) Never   (1) Less than monthly   (2) Monthly   (3) Weekly   (4) Daily or almost daily

8 How often during the past year have you been unable to remember what happened the night before because you had been drinking?

(0) Never   (1) Less than monthly   (2) Monthly   (3) Weekly   (4) Daily or almost daily

9 Have you or has someone else been injured as a result of your drinking?

(0) No   (2) Yes, but not in the past year   (4) Yes, during the past year

10 Has a relative or friend or a doctor or other health worker been concerned about your drinking or suggested you cut down?

(0) No   (2) Yes, but not in the past year   (4) Yes, during the past year

[a]Modified from the Mayfield D et al: The CAGE questionnaire: Validation of a new alcoholism screening instrument. Am J Psychiatry 1974;131:1121
[b]From Piccinelli M et al: Efficacy of the alcohol use disorders identification test as a screening tool for hazardous alcohol intake and related disorders in primary care: A validity study. BMJ 1997;314:420.

SCREENING INSTRUMENTS: COGNITIVE IMPAIRMENT

THE ANNOTATED MINI MENTAL STATE EXAMINATION (AMMSE)

MiniMental llc

> Suspect dementia
> when score ≤ 24.

NAME OF SUBJECT _____ Age _____

NAME OF EXAMINER _____ Years of School Completed ____

Approach the patient with respect and encouragement. Date of Examination _____

Ask: Do you have any trouble with your memory? ☐ Yes ☐ No

May I ask you some questions about your memory? ☐ Yes ☐ No

SCORE   ITEM

5 ( )   TIME ORIENTATION

Ask:

What is the year _____ (1), season _____ (1),

month of the year _____ (1), date _____ (1),

day of the week _____ (1)?

5 ( )   PLACE ORIENTATION

Ask:

Where are we now? What is the state _____ (1), city _____ (1),

part of the city_____ (1), building _____ (1),

floor of the building _____ (1)?

3 ( )   REGISTRATION OF THREE WORDS

Say: Listen carefully. I am going to say three words. You say them back after I stop.
Ready? Here they are...PONY (wait 1 second), QUARTER (wait 1 second), ORANGE
(wait 1 second). What were those words?

_____ (1)

_____ (1)

_____ (1)

Give 1 point for each correct answer, then repeat them until the patient learns all three.

5 ( )   SERIAL 7s AS A TEST OF ATTENTION AND CALCULATION

Ask: Subtract 7 from 100 and continue to subtract 7 form each subsequent remainder
until I tell you to stop. What is 100 take way 7? _____ (1)

Say:

Keep going. _____ (1), _____ (1),

_____ (1), _____ (1),

3 ( )   RECALL OF THREE WORDS

Ask:

What were those three words I asked you to remember?

Give one point for each correct answer. _____ (1),

_____ (1), _____ (1),

2 ( )   NAMING

Ask:

What is this? (show pencil) _____ (1). What is this? (show watch) _____ (1).

© 1975, 1998 MiniMental LLC

SCREENING INSTRUMENTS: COGNITIVE IMPAIRMENT

1 ( ) **REPETITION**
Say:
Now I am going to ask you to repeat what I say. Ready? No ifs, ands or buts.
Now you say that. _____ (1)

3 ( ) **COMPREHENSION**
Say:
Listen carefully because I am going to ask you to do something.
Take this paper in your left hand (1), fold it in half (1), and put it on the floor. (1)

1 ( ) **READING**
Say:
Please read the following and do what it says, but do not say it aloud. (1)

Close your eyes

1 ( ) **WRITING**
Say:
Please write a sentence. If the patient does not respond, say: Write about the weather. (1)
_____
_____

1 ( ) **DRAWING**
Say: Please copy this design.

TOTAL SCORE _____ Assess level of consciousness along a continuum

Alert	Drowsy	Stupor	Coma

	YES	NO
Cooperative:	☐	☐
Depressed:	☐	☐
Anxious:	☐	☐
Poor Vision:	☐	☐
Poor Hearing:	☐	☐
Native Language:		

	YES	NO
Deterioration from previous level of functioning:		
Family History of Dementia:	☐	☐
Head Trauma:	☐	☐
Stroke:	☐	☐
Alcohol Abuse:	☐	☐
Thyroid Disease:	☐	☐

FUNCTION BY PROXY
Please record date when patient was last able to perform the following tasks.
Ask caregiver if patient independently handles:

	YES	NO	DATE
Money/Bills:	☐	☐	_____
Medication:	☐	☐	_____
Transportation:	☐	☐	_____
Telephone:	☐	☐	_____

Source: Reproduced, with permission from "MINI-MENTAL STATE." A PRACTICAL METHOD FOR GRADING THE COGNITIVE STATE OF PATIENTS FOR THE CLINICIAN. Journal of Psychiatric Research 1975;12(3):189.
©1975, 1998 MiniMental LLC.

SCREENING INSTRUMENTS: DEPRESSION

SCREENING TESTS FOR DEPRESSION

Instrument Name	Screening Questions/Scoring	Threshold Score	Source
Beck Depression Inventory (Short Form)	See table below	0–4: none or minimal depression 5–7: mild depression 8–15: moderate depression > 15 = severe depression	Postgrad Med 1972;1:Dec:81
Geriatric Depression Scale	See table below	> 15 = depression	J Psychiatr Res 1983;17:37
PRIME-MD© (mood questions)	(1) During the past month, have you often been bothered by feeling down, depressed, or hopeless? (2) During the past month, have you often been bothered by little interest or pleasure in doing things?	"Yes" to either question[a]	JAMA 1994;272:1749 J Gen Intern Med 1997;12:439

[a]Sensitivity 86–96%, specificity 57–75%.

© Pfizer Inc.

SCREENING INSTRUMENTS: DEPRESSION

BECK DEPRESSION INVENTORY, SHORT FORM

Instructions: This is a questionnaire. On the questionnaire are groups of statements. Please read the entire group of statements in each category. Then pick out the one statement in that group that best describes the way you feel today, that is, *right now!* Circle the number beside the statement you have chosen. If several statements in the group seem to apply equally well, circle each one. Sum all numbers to calculate a score.

Be sure to read all the statements in each group before making your choice.

A. Sadness

3 I am so sad or unhappy that I can't stand it.

2 I am blue or sad all the time and I can't snap out of it.

1 I feel sad or blue.

0 I do not feel sad.

B. Pessimism

3 I feel that the future is hopeless and that things cannot improve.

2 I feel I have nothing to look forward to.

1 I feel discouraged about the future.

0 I am not particularly pessimistic or discouraged about the future.

C. Sense of failure

3 I feel I am a complete failure as a person (parent, husband, wife).

2 As I look back on my life, all I can see is a lot of failures.

1 I feel I have failed more than the average person.

0 I do not feel like a failure.

D. Dissatisfaction

3 I am dissatisfied with everything.

2 I don't get satisfaction out of anything anymore.

1 I don't enjoy things the way I used to.

0 I am not particularly dissatisfied.

E. Guilt

3 I feel as though I am very bad or worthless.

2 I feel quite guilty.

1 I feel bad or unworthy a good part of the time.

0 I don't feel particularly guilty.

F. Self-dislike

3 I hate myself.

2 I am disgusted with myself.

1 I am disappointed in myself.

0 I don't feel disappointed in myself.

G. Self-harm

3 I would kill myself if I had the chance.

2 I have definite plans about committing suicide.

1 I feel I would be better off dead.

0 I don't have any thoughts of harming myself.

H. Social withdrawal

3 I have lost all of my interest in other people and don't care about them at all.

2 I have lost most of my interest in other people and have little feeling for them.

1 I am less interested in other people than I used to be.

0 I have not lost interest in other people.

I. Indecisiveness

3 I can't make any decisions at all anymore.

2 I have great difficulty in making decisions.

1 I try to put of making decisions.

0 I make decisions about as well as ever.

J. Self-image change

3 I feel that I am ugly or repulsive-looking.

2 I feel that there are permanent changes in my appearance and they make me look unattractive.

1 I am worried that I am looking old or unattractive.

0 I don't feel that I look any worse than I used to.

SCREENING INSTRUMENTS: DEPRESSION

BECK DEPRESSION INVENTORY, SHORT FORM (CONTINUED)

K. Work difficulty
3 I can't do any work at all.
2 I have to push myself very hard to do anything.
1 It takes extra effort to get started at doing something.
0 I can work about as well as before.

L. Fatigability
3 I get too tired to do anything.

2 I get tired from doing anything.
1 I get tired more easily than I used to.
0 I don't get any more tired than usual.

M. Anorexia
3 I have no appetite at all anymore.
2 My appetite is much worse now.
1 My appetite is not as good as it used to be.
0 My appetite is no worse than usual.

Reproduced, with permission, from Beck AT, Beck RW: Screening depressed patients in family practice: A rapid technic. Postgrad Med 1972;52:81.

GERIATRIC DEPRESSION SCALE

Choose the best answer for how you felt over the past week

1.   Are you basically satisfied with your life? . . . .   yes / no
2.   Have you dropped many of your activities and interests?   yes / no
3.   Do you feel that your life is empty?   yes / no
4.   Do you often get bored?   yes / no
5.   Are you hopeful about the future? . . . .   yes / no
6.   Are you bothered by thoughts you can't get out of your head?   yes / no
7.   Are you in good spirits most of the time?   yes / no
8.   Are you afraid that something bad is going to happen to you?   yes / no
9.   Do you feel happy most of the time?   yes / no
10. Do you often feel helpless?. . . . .   yes / no
11. Do you often get restless and fidgety?   yes / no
12. Do you prefer to stay at home, rather than going out and doing new things?   yes / no
13. Do you frequently worry about the future?   yes / no
14. Do you feel you have more problems with memory than most?   yes / no
15. Do you think it is wonderful to be alive now? . . . .   yes / no

continued on next page

SCREENING INSTRUMENTS: DEPRESSION

GERIATRIC DEPRESSION SCALE (CONTINUED)

16.	Do you often feel downhearted and blue?	yes / no
17.	Do you feel pretty worthless the way you are now?	yes / no
18.	Do you worry a lot about the past?	yes / no
19.	Do you find life very exciting?	yes / no
20.	Is it hard for you to get started on new projects?	yes / no
21.	Do you feel full of energy?	yes / no
22.	Do you feel that your situation is hopeless?	yes / no
23.	Do you think that most people are better off than you are?	yes / no
24.	Do you frequently get upset over little things?	yes / no
25.	Do you frequently feel like crying?	yes / no
26.	Do you have trouble concentrating?	yes / no
27.	Do you enjoy getting up in the morning?	yes / no
28.	Do you prefer to avoid social gatherings?	yes / no
29.	Is it easy for you to make decisions?	yes / no
30.	Is your mind as clear as it used to be?	yes / no

One point for each response suggestive of depression. (Specifically "no" responses to questions 1, 5, 7, 9, 15, 19, 21, 27, 29, and 30, and "yes" responses to the remaining questions are suggestive of depression.) A score of ≥15 yields a sensitivity of 80% and a specificity of 100%, as a screening test for geriatric depression. (Clin Gerontologist 1982;1:37.)

Reproduced, with permission, from Yesavage JA et al: Development and validation of a geriatric depression screening scale: A preliminary report. J Psychiatr Res 1982-83;17:37.

PROCEDURE FOR FUNCTIONAL ASSESSMENT SCREENING IN THE ELDERLY

Target Area	Assessment Procedure	Abnormal Result	Suggested Intervention
Vision	Test each eye with Jaeger card while patient wears corrective lenses (if applicable).	Inability to read greater than 20/40	Refer to ophthalmologist.
Hearing	Whisper a short, easily answered question such as "What is your name?" in each ear while the examiner's face is out of direct view.	Inability to answer question	Examine auditory canals for cerumen and clean if necessary. Repeat test; if still abnormal in either ear, refer for audiometry and possible prosthesis.
Arm	Proximal: "Touch the back of your head with both hands." Distal: "Pick up the spoon."	Inability to do task	Examine the arm fully (muscle, joint, and nerve), paying attention to pain, weakness, limited range of motion. Consider referral for physical therapy.
Leg	Observe the patient after instructing as follows: "Rise from your chair, walk 10 feet, return, and sit down."	Inability to walk or transfer out of chair	Do full neurologic and musculoskeletal evaluation, paying attention to strength, pain, range of motion, balance, and gait. Consider referral for physical therapy.
Continence of urine	Ask, "Do you ever lose your urine and get wet?"	"Yes"	Ascertain frequency and amount. Search for remediable causes, including local irritations, polyuric states, and medications. Consider urologic referral.
Nutrition	Ask, "Without trying, have you lost 10 lb or more in the last 6 months?" Weigh the patient. Measure height.	"Yes" or weight is below acceptable range for height	Do appropriate medical evaluation.

continued on next page

PROCEDURE FOR FUNCTIONAL ASSESSMENT SCREENING IN THE ELDERLY (Continued)

Target Area	Assessment Procedure	Abnormal Result	Suggested Intervention
Mental status	Instruct as follows: "I am going to name three objects (pencil, truck, book). I will ask you to repeat their names now and then again a few minutes from now."	Inability to recall all three objects after 1 minute	Administer Folstein Mini-Mental Status Examination. If score is less than 24, search for causes of cognitive impairment. Ascertain onset, duration, and fluctuation of overt symptoms. Review medications. Assess consciousness and affect. Do appropriate laboratory tests.
Depression	Ask, "Do you often feel sad or depressed?" or "How are your spirits?"	"Yes" or "Not very good, I guess"	Administer Geriatric Depression Scale. If positive (score above 15), check for antihypertensive, psychotropic, or other pertinent medications. Consider appropriate pharmacologic or psychiatric treatment.
ADL-IADL[a]	Ask, "Can you get out of bed yourself?" "Can you dress yourself?" "Can you make your own meals?" "Can you do your own shopping?"	"No" to any question	Corroborate responses with patient's appearance; question family members if accuracy is uncertain. Determine reasons for the inability (motivation compared with physical limitation). Institute appropriate medical, social, or environmental interventions.
Home environment	Ask, "Do you have trouble with stairs inside or outside of your home?" Ask about potential hazards inside the home with bathtubs, rugs, or lighting.	"Yes"	Evaluate home safety and institute appropriate countermeasures.

	PROCEDURE FOR FUNCTIONAL ASSESSMENT SCREENING IN THE ELDERLY (Continued)		
Target Area	**Assessment Procedure**	**Abnormal Result**	**Suggested Intervention**
Social support	Ask, "Who would be able to help you in case of illness or emergency?"	. . .	List identified persons in the medical record. Become familiar with available resources for the elderly in the community.

[a]Activities of daily living–instrumental activities of daily living.

Source; Modified from Lachs MS et al: A simple procedure for screening for functional disability in elderly patients. Ann Intern Med 1990;112:699.

95TH PERCENTILE OF BLOOD PRESSURE FOR BOYS AND GIRLS: BOYS

Age (y)	Systolic BP (mm Hg) by percentile of height							Diastolic BP (mm Hg) by percentile of height						
	5%	10%	25%	50%	75%	90%	95%	5%	10%	25%	50%	75%	90%	95%
3	105	106	107	109	111	112	113	63	63	64	65	66	67	68
4	107	108	109	111	113	114	115	67	68	68	69	70	71	72
5	108	109	111	113	114	116	117	71	71	72	73	74	75	76
6	109	110	112	114	116	117	118	74	75	75	76	77	78	79
7	110	111	113	115	117	118	119	77	77	78	79	80	81	81
8	112	113	114	116	118	119	120	79	79	80	81	82	83	83
9	113	114	116	118	119	121	122	80	81	81	82	83	84	85
10	115	116	117	119	121	123	123	81	82	83	83	84	85	86
11	117	118	119	121	123	125	125	82	82	83	84	85	86	87
12	119	120	122	124	125	127	128	83	83	84	85	86	87	87
13	121	122	124	126	128	129	130	83	83	84	85	86	87	88
14	124	125	127	129	131	132	133	83	84	85	86	87	87	88
15	127	128	130	132	133	135	136	84	85	86	86	87	88	89
16	130	131	133	134	136	138	138	86	86	87	88	89	90	90
17	132	133	135	137	139	140	141	88	88	89	90	91	92	93

95TH PERCENTILE OF BLOOD PRESSURE FOR BOYS AND GIRLS: GIRLS

Age (y)	Systolic BP (mm Hg) by percentile of height							Diastolic BP (mm Hg) by percentile of height						
	5%	10%	25%	50%	75%	90%	95%	5%	10%	25%	50%	75%	90%	95%
3	104	104	106	107	108	109	110	65	65	66	66	67	68	68
4	105	106	107	108	109	111	111	68	68	69	69	70	71	71
5	107	107	108	110	111	112	113	71	71	71	72	73	74	74
6	108	109	110	111	113	114	114	73	73	74	74	75	76	76
7	110	110	112	113	114	115	116	75	75	75	76	77	78	78
8	112	112	113	115	116	117	118	76	76	77	78	79	79	80
9	114	114	116	117	118	119	120	78	78	79	79	80	81	81
10	116	116	118	119	120	122	122	79	79	80	81	81	82	83
11	118	118	120	121	122	124	124	81	81	81	82	83	83	84
12	120	120	122	123	125	126	126	82	82	82	83	84	85	85
13	122	122	124	125	126	128	128	83	83	84	84	85	86	86
14	124	124	126	127	128	129	130	84	84	85	85	86	87	87
15	125	125	127	128	130	131	131	85	85	85	86	87	88	88
16	126	126	127	128	130	132	132	85	85	86	87	87	88	88
17	127	127	128	130	131	132	133	85	86	86	87	88	88	89

Source: Adapted, with permission, from Rosner B et al: Blood pressure nomograms for children and adolescents, by height, sex, and age, in the United States. J Pediatr 1993;123:874.

BODY MASS INDEX CONVERSION TABLE		
	BMI 25 kg/m^2	BMI 27 kg/m^2	BMI 30 kg/m^2
Height in inches (cm)	Body weight in pounds (kg)		
58 (147.32)	119 (53.98)	129 (58.51)	143 (64.86)
59 (149.86)	124 (56.25)	133 (60.33)	148 (67.13)
60 (152.40)	128 (58.06)	138 (62.60)	153 (69.40)
61 (154.94)	132 (59.87)	143 (64.86)	158 (71.67)
62 (157.48)	136 (61.69)	147 (66.68)	164 (74.39)
63 (160.02)	141 (63.96)	152 (68.95)	169 (76.66)
64 (162.56)	145 (65.77)	157 (71.22)	174 (78.93)
65 (165.10)	150 (68.04)	162 (73.48)	180 (81.65)
66 (167.64)	155 (70.31)	167 (75.75)	186 (84.37)
67 (170.18)	159 (72.12)	172 (78.02)	191 (86.64)
68 (172.72)	164 (74.39)	177 (80.29)	197 (89.36)
69 (175.26)	169 (76.66)	182 (82.56)	203 (92.08)
70 (177.80)	174 (78.93)	188 (85.28)	207 (93.90)
71 (180.34)	179 (81.19)	193 (87.54)	215 (97.52)
72 (182.88)	184 (83.46)	199 (90.27)	221 (100.25)
73 (185.42)	189 (85.73)	204 (92.53)	227 (102.97)
74 (187.96)	194 (88.00)	210 (95.26)	233 (105.69)
75 (190.50)	200 (90.72)	216 (97.98)	240 (108.86)
76 (193.04)	205 (92.99)	221 (100.25)	246 (111.59)

Metric conversion formula = weight (kg)/height (m^2)	**Non-metric conversion formula =** [weight (pounds)/height (inches)^2] × 704.5
Example of BMI calculation:	Example of BMI calculation:
A person who weighs 78.93 kilograms and is 177 centimeters tall has a BMI of 25:	A person who weighs 164 pounds and is 68 inches (or 5′ 8″) tall has a BMI of 25:
weight (78.93 kg)/height (1.77 m)^2 = 25	[weight (164 pounds)/height (68 inches)^2] × 704.5 = 25

Source: Adapted from NHLBI Obesity Guidelines in Adults, 1998

RECOMMENDED CHILDHOOD IMMUNIZATION SCHEDULE (ACIP)

Vaccine	Birth	1 mo	2 mo	4 mo	6 mo	12 mo	15 mo	18 mo	4–6 y	11–12 y	14–16 y
						Age[a]					
HBV[b]	Hep B	Hep B			Hep B					Hep B[c]	
DTaP[d]			DTaP	DTaP	DTaP		DTaP	DTaP	DTaP	Td	
HiB[e]			Hib	Hib	Hib	Hib					
Poliomyelitis virus[f]			IPV	IPV	IPV				IPV		
MMR[g]						MMR			MMR	MMR[c]	
Varicella[h]						Var		Var		Var[c]	
HAV									Age ≥ 2 years, high risk[i]		
Streptococcus pneumoniae									Age ≥ 2 years, high risk[j]		
Influenza					For high risk[k]						

Range of acceptable ages for vaccination.

[a]This schedule indicates the recommended ages for routine administration of currently licensed childhood vaccines. Any dose not given at the recommended age should be given as a "catch-up" vaccination at any subsequent visit when indicated and feasible. Combination vaccines may be used whenever any components of the combination are indicated and its other components are not contraindicated. Providers should consult the manufacturers' package inserts for detailed recommendations.

[b]*Infants of HBsAg-negative mothers:* Second dose should be given at least 1 month after the first. Third dose should be at least 4 months after the first dose and at least 2 months after the second dose, but not before age 6 months. *Infants of HBsAg-positive mothers:* Give hepatitis B vaccine and hepatitis B immune globulin within 12 hours of birth, second dose at ages 1–2 months, and third dose at age 6 months. *Infants for whom maternal HBsAg status is unknown:* Give hepatitis B vaccine within 12 hours of birth. Determine maternal HBsAg status: If positive, provide hepatitis B immune globulin as soon as possible (no later than age 1 week). All children and adolescents (age 18 years) who have not been vaccinated against hepatitis B may begin the series during any visit. Special efforts should be made to vaccinate children who were born in or whose parents were born in areas of the world where HBV infection is moderately or highly endemic.

[c]Vaccines to be assessed and administered if necessary.

[d]DTaP is the preferred vaccine for all doses in the vaccination series, including completion of the series in children who have received 1 or more doses of whole-cell DTP. The fourth dose may be administered as early as age 12 months, provided 6 months have elapsed since the third dose, particularly if the child is unlikely to return at ages 15–18 months. Td is recommended at ages 11–12 years if at least 5 years have elapsed since the last dose of DTP, DTaP, or DT. Subsequent routine Td boosters are recommended every 10 years.

[e]The Hib conjugate vaccines (PRP-OMP) is administered at ages 2 and 4 months, a dose at age 6 months is not required.

[f]Two poliovirus vaccines are licensed in the United States: IPV and OPV OPV is no longer recommended for the first 2 doses of the schedule and is acceptable only in special circumstances (eg, children of parents who do not accept the recommended number of injections, late initiation of vaccination that would require an unacceptable number of injections, and imminent travel to areas where poliomyelitis is endemic). OPV remains the vaccine of choice for mass vaccination campaigns to control outbreaks of wild poliovirus.

[g]The second dose of MMR is recommended routinely at ages 4–6 years but may be administered during any visit, provided that at least 4 weeks have elapsed since receipt of the first dose and that both doses are administered beginning at or after age 12 months. Those who have not previously received the second dose should complete the schedule no later than the routine visit at ages 11–12 years.

[h]Varicella vaccine is recommended at any visit on or after the first birthday for susceptible children (ie, those who lack a reliable history of chickenpox and who have not been vaccinated). Susceptible persons age ≥ 13 years should receive 2 doses given at least 4 weeks apart.

[i]High risk: persons living in, traveling to, or working in areas where the disease is endemic and periodic outbreaks occur; institutionalized persons; men who have sex with men; injection drug users; military personnel; and certain hospital and laboratory workers. Schedule: 3 doses, with second and third doses given 1 and 6–12 months after the first dose. If patient requires immediate protection against HAV, administer immune globulin simultaneously with the first vaccine dose.

[j]High risk: chronic cardiac or pulmonary disease, diabetes mellitus, anatomic asplenia, special environments with increased risk of pneumococcal disease (eg, certain Native American and Alaska Native populations), cirrhosis, chronic renal failure, nephrotic syndrome, sickle cell disease, metastatic or hematologic malignancy, and acquired or congenital immunodeficiency. Routine revaccination is not recommended but may be appropriate to consider in individuals at highest risk for morbidity and mortality from pneumococcal disease (ie, asplenia, immunocompromise) who were vaccinated > 5 years previously.

[k]High risk: residents of chronic care facilities and patients with chronic cardiopulmonary disorders, metabolic diseases (including diabetes mellitus), hemoglobinopathies, immunosuppression, and renal dysfunction.

Source: Modified from Recommended childhood immunization schedule–United States. MMWR Morb Mortal Wkly Rep 1999;48:12.

RECOMMENDED ADULT IMMUNIZATION SCHEDULE

Vaccine	Age 18–24 y	25–34 y	35–44 y	45–54 y	55–64 y	65–74 y	≥75 y
HBV[a]	If not previously vaccinated	For high risk[b]					
DTP	Td booster every 10 years					Td booster at age 65 years	
HAV	For high risk[c]						
Streptococcus pneumoniae	For high risk[d]					Once	
Influenza	For high risk[e]					Annually	
MMR[f]	Women of childbearing age[f]						
Varicella	Two doses at least 4 weeks apart for susceptible persons[g]						

☐ Range of acceptable ages for vaccination.

☐ Recommended schedule: initial vaccine, then repeat at 1 and 6 months.

[a] Recommended schedule: initial vaccine, then repeat at 1 and 6 months.

[b] High risk: men who have had sex with men, injection drug users and their sexual partners, patients with a history of sexual activity with multiple partners or history of another sexually transmitted disease, international travelers to countries where HBV is of high or intermediate endemicity, recipients of certain blood products (including hemodialysis patients), and persons in health-related jobs with frequent exposure to blood or blood products. Consider testing antibody response in individuals at very high risk of HBV who are likely to have inadequate antibody response (ie, chronic renal dialysis patients, injection drug users, and those with HIV infection).

cHigh risk: persons living in, traveling to, or working in areas where the disease is endemic and periodic outbreaks occur; institutionalized persons; men who have sex with men; injection drug users; military personnel; and certain hospital and laboratory workers. Schedule: 2 doses, with the second dose 6–12 months after the first. If patient requires immediate protection against HAV, administer immune globulin simultaneously with the first vaccine dose.

dHigh risk: institutionalized persons age ≥ 50 years, chronic cardiac or pulmonary disease, diabetes mellitus, anatomic asplenia, special environments with increased risk of pneumococcal disease (eg, certain Native American and Alaska Native populations), alcoholism, cirrhosis, chronic renal failure, nephrotic syndrome, sickle cell disease, multiple myeloma, metastatic or hematologic malignancy, and acquired or congenital immunodeficiency. Routine revaccination is not recommended but may be appropriate to consider in individuals at highest risk for morbidity and mortality from pneumococcal disease (ie, functional or anatomic asplenia, immunocompromised patients) who were vaccinated > 5 years previously, or if age was < 65 years at the time of primary vaccination.

eHigh risk: residents of chronic care facilities, chronic cardiopulmonary disorders, metabolic diseases (including diabetes mellitus), hemoglobinopathies, immunosuppression, renal dysfunction, and health care providers for and household members of high-risk patients.

fObtain history of vaccination and serology, or offer vaccination. Do not administer rubella vaccine to pregnant women. Women receiving rubella vaccine should not become pregnant for 3 months after vaccination.

gSusceptible persons are those who lack a reliable history of chickenpox or were never vaccinated. Consider offering serologic testing to adolescents and adults without a reliable history of infection or immunization.

MANAGEMENT ALGORITHMS: ASTHMA

STEPWISE APPROACH FOR MANAGING ASTHMA IN ADULTS AND CHILDREN OLDER THAN 5 YEARS OF AGE

Goals of Asthma Treatment

- Prevent chronic and troublesome symptoms (eg, coughing or breathlessness in the night, in the early morning, or after exertion).
- Maintain (near) "normal" pulmonary function.
- Maintain normal activity levels (including exercise and other physical activity).
- Prevent recurrent exacerbations of asthma and minimize the need for emergency department visits or hospitalizations.
- Provide optimal pharmacotherapy with minimal or no adverse effects.
- Meet patients' and families' expectations of and satisfaction with asthma care.

Classify Severity of Asthma

	Clinical Features Before Treatment[a]		
	Symptoms[b]	Nighttime Symptoms	Lung Function
STEP 4 Severe Persistent	• Continual symptoms • Limited physical activity • Frequent exacerbations	Frequent	• FEV_1 or PEF ≤ 60% predicted • PEF variability > 30%
STEP 3 Moderate Persistent	• Daily symptoms • Daily use of inhaled short-acting beta₂-agonist • Exacerbations affect activity • Exacerbations ≥ 2 times a week; may last days	> 1 time a week	• FEV_1 or PEF > 60%–< 80% predicted • PEF variability > 30%
STEP 2 Mild Persistent	• Symptoms > 2 times a week but < 1 time a day • Exacerbations may affect activity	> 2 times a month	• FEV_1 or PEF ≥ 80% predicted • PEF variability 20–30%

MANAGEMENT ALGORITHMS: ASTHMA

STEPWISE APPROACH FOR MANAGING ASTHMA IN ADULTS AND CHILDREN OLDER THAN 5 YEARS OF AGE (CONTINUED)

Classify Severity of Asthma

	Clinical Features Before Treatment[a]		
	Symptoms[b]	Nighttime Symptoms	Lung Function
STEP 1 Mild Intermittent	• Symptoms ≤ 2 times a week • Asymptomatic and normal PEF between exacerbations • Exacerbations brief (from a few hours to a few days); intensity may vary	≤ 2 times a month	• FEV$_1$ or PEF ≥ 80% predicted • PEF variability < 20%

[a]The presence of one of the features of severity is sufficient to place a patient in that category. An individual should be assigned to the most severe grade in which any feature occurs. The characteristics noted in this table are general and may overlap because asthma is highly variable. Furthermore, an individual's classification may change over time.

[b]Patients at any level of severity can have mild, moderate, or severe exacerbations. Some patients with intermittent asthma experience severe and life-threatening exacerbations separated by long periods of normal lung function and no symptoms.

FEV$_1$ = forced expiratory volume in 1 second; PEF = peak expiratory flow.

Source: National Heart, Lung and Blood Institute; NIH. http://www.nhlbi.gov/nhlbi/lung/asthma/prof/practgde.htm

MANAGEMENT ALGORITHMS: ASTHMA

STEPWISE APPROACH FOR MANAGING ASTHMA IN ADULTS AND CHILDREN OLDER THAN 5 YEARS OF AGE: TREATMENT

	Long-Term Control	Quick Relief	Education
STEP 4 Severe Persistent	Daily medications: • Anti-inflammatory: inhaled corticosteroid (high dose) AND • Long-acting bronchodilator: either long-acting inhaled beta$_2$-agonist, sustained-release theophylline, or long-acting beta$_2$-agonist tablets AND • Corticosteroid tablets or syrup long term (make repeat attempts to reduce systemic steroids and maintain control with high-dose inhaled steroids)	• Short-acting bronchodilator: inhaled beta$_2$-agonists as needed for symptoms • Intensity of treatment will depend on severity of exacerbation. • Use of short-acting inhaled beta$_2$-agonists on a daily basis, or increasing use, indicates the need for additional long-term-control therapy.	Steps 2 and 3 actions plus: • Refer to individual education/counseling.

MANAGEMENT ALGORITHMS: ASTHMA

STEPWISE APPROACH FOR MANAGING ASTHMA IN ADULTS AND CHILDREN OLDER THAN 5 YEARS OF AGE: TREATMENT (CONTINUED)

STEP 3
Moderate Persistent
	Daily medication:
	• Either
	  Anti-inflammatory: inhaled corticosteroid (medium dose)
	OR
	  Inhaled corticosteroid (low–medium dose) and add a long-acting bronchodilator, especially for nighttime symptoms; either long-acting inhaled beta$_2$-agonist, sustained-release theophylline, or long-acting beta$_2$-agonist tablets
	• If needed
	  Anti-inflammatory: inhaled corticosteroids (medium–high dose)
	AND
	  Long-acting bronchodilator: either long-acting inhaled beta$_2$-agonist, sustained-release theophylline, or long-acting beta$_2$-agonist tablets
		• Short-acting bronchodilator: inhaled beta$_2$-agonists as needed for symptoms
		• Intensity of treatment will depend on severity of exacerbation.
		• Use of short-acting inhaled beta$_2$-agonists on a daily basis, or increasing use, indicates the need for additional long-term-control therapy.
			Step 1 actions plus:
			• Teach self-monitoring.
			• Refer to group education if available.
			• Review and update self-management plan.

MANAGEMENT ALGORITHMS: ASTHMA

STEPWISE APPROACH FOR MANAGING ASTHMA IN ADULTS AND CHILDREN OLDER THAN 5 YEARS OF AGE: TREATMENT (CONTINUED)

	Long-Term Control	Quick Relief	Education
STEP 2 Mild Persistent	One daily medication: • Anti-inflammatory: either inhaled corticosteroid (low doses) or cromolyn or nedocromil (children usually begin with a trial of cromolyn or nedocromil) • Sustained-release theophylline to serum concentration of 5–15 μg/mL is an alternative, but not preferred, therapy. Zafirlukast or zileuton may also be considered for patients > 12 years of age, although their position in therapy is not fully established.	• Short-acting bronchodilator: inhaled beta₂-agonists as needed for symptoms • Intensity of treatment will depend on severity of exacerbation. • Use of short-acting inhaled beta₂-agonists on a daily basis, or increasing use, indicates the need for additional long-term-control therapy.	Step 1 actions plus: • Teach self-monitoring. • Refer to group education if available. • Review and update self-management plan.
STEP 1 Mild Intermittent	• No daily medication needed	• Short-acting bronchodilator: inhaled beta₂-agonists as needed for symptoms • Intensity of treatment will depend on severity of exacerbation. • Use of short-acting inhaled beta₂-agonists more than 2 times a week may indicate the need to initiate long-term-control therapy.	• Teach basic facts about asthma. • Teach inhaler/spacer/holding chamber technique. • Discuss roles of medications. • Develop self-management plan. • Develop action plan for when and how to take rescue actions, especially for patients with a history of severe exacerbations. • Discuss appropriate environmental control measures to avoid exposure to known allergens and irritants.

MANAGEMENT ALGORITHMS: ASTHMA

STEPWISE APPROACH FOR MANAGING ASTHMA IN ADULTS AND CHILDREN OLDER THAN 5 YEARS OF AGE: TREATMENT (CONTINUED)

Step down	Step up
Review treatment every 1–6 months; a gradual stepwise reduction in treatment may be possible.	If control is not maintained, consider step up. First, review patient medication technique, adherence, and environmental control (avoidance of allergens or other factors that contribute to asthma severity).

NOTE:

• The stepwise approach presents general guidelines to assist clinical decision making; it is not intended to be a specific prescription. Asthma is highly variable; clinicians should tailor specific medication plans to the needs and circumstances of individual patients.

• Gain control as quickly as possible; then decrease treatment to the least medication necessary to maintain control. Gaining control may be accomplished by either starting treatment at the step most appropriate to the initial severity of the condition or starting at a higher level of therapy (eg, a course of systemic corticosteroids or higher dose of inhaled corticosteroids).

• A rescue course of systemic corticosteroids may be needed at any time and at any step.

• Some patients with intermittent asthma experience severe and life-threatening exacerbations separated by long periods of normal lung function and no symptoms. This may be especially common with exacerbations provoked by respiratory infections. A short course of systemic corticosteroids is recommended.

• At each step, patients should control their environment to avoid or control factors that make their asthma worse (eg, allergens, irritants); this requires specific diagnosis and education.

• Referral to an asthma specialist for consultation or comanagement is *recommended* if there are difficulties achieving or maintaining control of asthma or if the patient requires step 4 care. Referral may be *considered* if the patient requires step 3 care.

Source: National Heart, Lung and Blood Institute; NIH. http://www.nhlbi.gov/lung/asthma/prof/practgde.htm

MANAGEMENT ALGORITHMS: ATRIAL FIBRILLATION

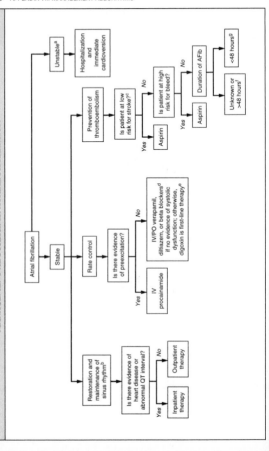

Atrial fibrillation

→ Stable

→ Unstable[a]
→ Hospitalization and immediate cardioversion

Stable branch:

Restoration and maintenance of sinus rhythm[b]
- Is there evidence of heart disease or abnormal QT interval?
  - Yes → Inpatient therapy
  - No → Outpatient therapy

Rate control
- Is there evidence of preexcitation?
  - Yes → IV procainamide
  - No → IV/PO verapamil, diltiazem, or beta blockers[d] if no evidence of systolic dysfunction; otherwise, digoxin is first-line therapy[e]

Prevention of thromboembolism
- Is the patient at low risk for stroke?[c]
  - Yes → Aspirin
  - No → Is patient at high risk for bleed?
    - Yes → Aspirin
    - No → Duration of AFib
      - <48 hours[g]
      - Unknown or >48 hours[i]

(Continued)

[a] Evidence of Wolff-Parkinson-White syndrome or pre-excitation, hypotension, or congestive heart failure.

[b] Maintenance of sinus rhythm after cardioversion is improved by treatment with quinidine, procainamide, disopyramide, propafenone, sotalol, flecainide, or amiodarone. Selection of an antiarrhythmic agent should take into account the patient's liver and renal function, comorbidities, and systolic function.

[c] Patients at high stroke risk (thromboembolic rates > 5% per year) include those with a history of hypertension, prior stroke/transient ischemic attack, diabetes, age > 65 years, impaired systolic function, and enlarged left atrial size. Low-risk patients have a thromboembolic risk of 1–1.5% per year. (Arch Intern Med 1994;154:1449; Ann Intern Med 1992;116:1).

[d] Beta-blockers are especially effective in the setting of thyrotoxicosis or increased sympathetic tone (eg, alcohol withdrawal).

[e] If rate is difficult to control with pharmacologic therapy, consider AV node ablation or modification.

[f] Two options: (1) Anticoagulate x 3 weeks (INR 2.0–3.0), followed by electrical/pharmacologic cardioversion; if successful, continue anticoagulation for an additional 4 weeks; or (2) begin IV heparin and perform transesophageal echocardiography; if no atrial thrombus, then perform cardioversion followed by 4 weeks of anticoagulation. Patients age > 75 years should be monitored more closely for therapeutic INR and perhaps be kept closer to 2.0.

[g] Cardioversion can be performed. There are few data to guide the need for anticoagulation.

AFib = atrial fibrillation

Source: Modified from Prystowsky EN et al: Management of patients with atrial fibrillation. A Statement for Healthcare Professionals. From the Subcommittee on Electrocardiography and Electrophysiology, American Heart Association. Circulation 1996;93:1262.

MANAGEMENT ALGORITHMS: DEPRESSION

OVERVIEW OF TREATMENT FOR DEPRESSION

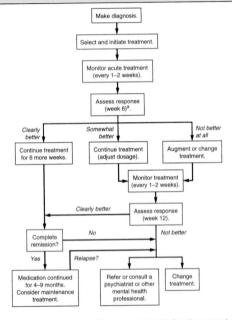

[a]Times of assessment (weeks 6 and 12) rest on very modest data. It may be necessary to revise the treatment plan earlier for patients who fail to respond at all.

Source: Reproduced, with permission, from Agency for Health Care Policy and Research: Depression in Primary Care. Vol. 2: Treatment of Major Depression. United States Department of Health and Human Services, 1993.

MANAGEMENT ALGORITHMS: DIABETES MELLITUS

MANAGEMENT OF HYPERGLYCEMIA[a]

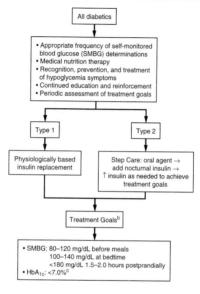

All diabetics

- Appropriate frequency of self-monitored blood glucose (SMBG) determinations
- Medical nutrition therapy
- Recognition, prevention, and treatment of hypoglycemia symptoms
- Continued education and reinforcement
- Periodic assessment of treatment goals

Type 1

Type 2

Physiologically based insulin replacement

Step Care: oral agent → add nocturnal insulin → ↑ insulin as needed to achieve treatment goals

Treatment Goals[b]

- SMBG: 80–120 mg/dL before meals
  100–140 mg/dL at bedtime
  <180 mg/dL 1.5–2.0 hours postprandially
- HbA$_{1c}$: <7.0%[c]

[a]Adapted form American Diabetes Association Position Statement "Standards of Medical Care for Patients With Diabetes Mellitus." Last updated January 1999. (http://www.diabetes.org/DiabetesCare/Supplement199/S32.htm)

[b]These are generalized goals. They do not apply to pregnant adults. One should modify individual treatment goals to take into account risk for hypoglycemia, very young or old age, end-stage renal disease, advanced cardiovascular or cerebrovascular disease, or other diseases that decrease life expectancy.

[c]Based on results of the Diabetes Control and Complications Trial (DCCT) (Type 1) and the United Kingdom Prospective Diabetes Study (UKPDS) (Type 2).

MANAGEMENT ALGORITHMS: DIABETES MELLITUS

PREVENTION & TREATMENT OF DIABETIC COMPLICATIONS

Complication	Goal	Monitoring	Action if Goal Not Met
Hyperglycemia	HbA$_{1C}$ < 7.0%	HbA$_{1C}$ ≥ every six months	See management, Appendix VII
Retinopathy	Prevent vision loss	Annual retinal exam[a]	Laser treatment
Neuropathy	Prevent foot complications	Annual foot exam[b]	Examine feet at every visit
Nephropathy	Prevent renal failure	Annual urinary protein determination[c]	See below[d]
Hypertension	Adult: BP < 130/85 mm Hg Elderly: SBP < 160 mm Hg	Annual BP determination	See JNC VI, Appendix VII
Hyperlipidemia	LDL < 100 mg/dL.	Annual determination unless low risk	Weight loss; increase in physical activity; nutrition therapy; follow NCEP recommendations for pharmacologic treatment, Appendix VII

[a]Dilated eye exam or 7-field 30-degree fundus photography by ophthalmologist or optometrist.
[b]Includes evaluation of protective sensation, vascular status, and inspection for foot deformities or ulcers.

[c]Albuminuria Thresholds

Category	24-h collection (mg/24 h)	Timed collection (µg/min)	Spot collection (µg/creatinine)
Normal	<30	<20	<30
Microalbuminuria	30–300	20–200	30–300
Clinical albuminuria	>300	>200	>300

Because of variability in urinary albumin excretion, two of three specimens collected within a 3- to 6-month period should be abnormal before considering a patient to have crossed one of these diagnostic thresholds. Exercise within 24 h, infection, fever, congestive heart failure, marked hyperglycemia, and marked hypertension may elevate urinary albumin excretion over baseline values.

MANAGEMENT ALGORITHMS: DIABETES MELLITUS

PREVENTION & TREATMENT OF DIABETIC COMPLICATIONS (CONTINUED)

[c]Microalbuminuria treatment: if type 1: ACE inhibitor; if type 2: individualize decision. Clinical albuminuria treatment: (1) Achieve BP < 130/85 mm Hg; (2) use ACE inhibitor; (3) improve glycemic control; and (4) decrease protein to 10% of dietary intake. Refer to nephrologist if: glomerular filtration rate < 70 ml/min, creatinine > 2.0 mg/dL, or when management of hypertension or hyperkalemia is difficult.

Source: Adapted from American Diabetes Association Position Statement "Standards of Medical Care for Patients With Diabetes Mellitus." Last updated January 1999 (http://www.diabetes.org/DiabetesCare/Supplement 199/S32.htm)

MANAGEMENT ALGORITHMS: HORMONE REPLACEMENT THERAPY

RISKS AND BENEFITS OF HORMONE REPLACEMENT THERAPY (HRT)[a]

	Risk for Untreated Women (Average)	Risk/Benefit with HRT
Breast Cancer	Lifetime risk 10%	No increased risk with short-term (< 5 years) therapy; risk may be increased with long-term therapy. A recent study suggests that an estrogen-progestin regimen (increased RR = 0.12 per year of treatment) increases breast cancer risk beyond that associated with estrogen alone (increased RR = 0.03 per year of treatment) among women with BMI ≤ 24.4 kg/m^2 (JAMA 2000; 283:485)
Coronary Heart Disease (CHD)	46% lifetime probability of developing and 31% risk of dying from CHD. After age 60 years, CHD is the primary cause of death for women.	There is 3–50% less CHD among women who have ever used estrogens, compared with those who have never used them. The only prospective trial of HRT showed no benefit of HRT on CHD events in women with a history of CAD (i.e. secondary prevention). (JAMA 1998;280:605)
Endometrial cancer	Lifetime risk 2.6%	With unopposed estrogen, risk is increased 4- to 11-fold. Addition of progestins for at least 10 days per month prevents development of the endometrial hyperplasia associated with unopposed estrogen use.
Osteoporosis	15% lifetime probability of hip fracture (for white women)	Rates of vertebral, wrist, and hip fractures can be reduced by 50–80% after 6–10 years of therapy.

[a]To aid in individualized patient counseling.

Source: Modified, with permission, from Goroll AH, May LA, Mulley AG Jr (editors): Primary Care Medicine: Office Evaluation and Management of the Adult Patient, 3rd ed. JB Lippincott, 1995. Rosenfeld JA (editor): Women's Health in Primary Care. Williams & Wilkins, 1997.

MANAGEMENT ALGORITHMS: HORMONE REPLACEMENT THERAPY

HRT TREATMENT REGIMENS FOR WOMEN WITH INTACT UTERI[a]

HRT	Days of Month	Comments
Estrogen Progestin None	1–25 14–25 26–30	97% have withdrawal bleeding until at least age 60 years; after age 65 only 60% continue to bleed.
Estrogen Progestin	1–30 14–25	Avoids estrogen deficiency symptoms.
Estrogen Progestin	1–30 1–30	Avoids cyclic bleeding. During the first 4–6 months, 35% experience unpredictable spotting and bleeding; by 6 months, 60–65% are amenorrheic.
Estrogen Progestin	1–25 1–25	May provide greater endometrial protection because stopping progestin allows endometrial shedding. Less breakthrough bleeding after the first month than with continuous combined therapy; 75% are amenorrheic by 4 months.

[a]For women without a uterus, progestin is not needed.

Source: Modified, with permission, from Goroll AH, May LA, Mulley AG Jr (editors): *Primary Care Medicine: Office Evaluation and Management of the Adult Patient,* 3rd ed. JB Lippincott, 1995. Rosenfeld JA (editor): *Women's Health in Primary Care.* Williams & Wilkins, 1997.

MANAGEMENT ALGORITHMS: HORMONE REPLACEMENT THERAPY

HRT: MANAGEMENT OF SYMPTOMS AND SIDE EFFECTS

Symptom/Side Effect	Suggested Intervention
Abdominal bloating	Try lower dose or different progestin. Try hydrochlorothiazide during progestin therapy.
Bleeding on unopposed estrogen or irregular bleeding on combination therapy	Endometrial biopsy
Breakthrough bleeding on combination therapy	Increase progestin dose at 3-month intervals.
Breast tenderness	Lower estrogen dose. Try a different progestin. Consider use of hydrochlorothiazide. Avoid caffeine. Try vitamin E. Evaluate if condition persists.
Decreased libido	Try androgen–estrogen combination.
Migraine headaches	Try transdermal patch. Stop HRT if headaches continue.
Nausea	Often decreases with time. Take medication with food or at bedtime. Try lower doses or transdermal patches.
Persistent menopausal symptoms	Increase estrogen dose or try different estrogen or different delivery system.
Urogenital atrophy	Use topical estrogen. Initiate with daily administration for 3–4 weeks, then decrease to twice weekly.

Source: Modified from Gorell AH, May LA, Mulley AG Jr (editors): Office Evaluation and Management of the Adult Patient, 3rd ed. JB Lippincott, 1995. Rosenfeld JA (editor): Women's Health in Primary Care. Williams & Wilkins, 1997.

MANAGEMENT ALGORITHMS: HYPERLIPIDEMIA

CHOLESTEROL MANAGEMENT

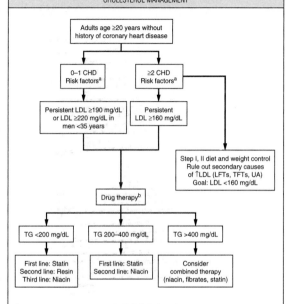

Adults age ≥20 years without history of coronary heart disease

0–1 CHD Risk factors[a]

≥2 CHD Risk factors[a]

Persistent LDL ≥190 mg/dL or LDL ≥220 mg/dL in men <35 years

Persistent LDL ≥160 mg/dL

Step I, II diet and weight control
Rule out secondary causes of ↑LDL (LFTs, TFTs, UA)
Goal: LDL <160 mg/dL

Drug therapy[b]

TG <200 mg/dL

TG 200–400 mg/dL

TG >400 mg/dL

First line: Statin
Second line: Resin
Third line: Niacin

First line: Statin
Second line: Niacin

Consider combined therapy (niacin, fibrates, statin)

[a]Age (men ≥45 years, women ≥55 years or postmenopausal), hypertension, diabetes, smoking, HDL <35 mg/dL, family history of CHD in first-degree relative (male relatives <55 years, female relatives <65 years). For HDL ≥60 mg/dL, subtract 1 risk factor from above.
[b]If HDL <35 mg/dL, consider niacin (except patients with diabetes).
CHD = coronary heart disease; LDL = low-density lipoprotein; LFT = liver function test; TFT = thyroid function test; UA = urinalysis; TG = triglyceride; HDL = high-density lipoprotein
Source: Modified from AHA Scientific Statement. Guide to Primary Prevention of Cardiovascular Diseases. Circulation 1997;95:2330.

MANAGEMENT ALGORITHMS: HYPERTENSION

ALGORITHM FOR THE TREATMENT OF HYPERTENSION

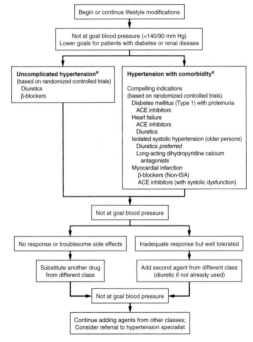

Begin or continue lifestyle modifications

Not at goal blood pressure (<140/90 mm Hg)
Lower goals for patients with diabetes or renal disease

Uncomplicated hypertension[a]
(based on randomized controlled trials)
Diuretics
β-blockers

Hypertension with comorbidity[a]

Compelling indications
(based on randomized controlled trials)
Diabetes mellitus (Type 1) with proteinuria
ACE inhibitors
Heart failure
ACE inhibitors
Diuretics
Isolated systolic hypertension (older persons)
Diuretics *preferred*
Long-acting dihydropyridine calcium
antagonists
Myocardial infarction
β-blockers (Non-ISA)
ACE inhibitors (with systolic dysfunction)

Not at goal blood pressure

No response or troublesome side effects

Inadequate response but well tolerated

Substitute another drug
from different class

Add second agent from different class
(diuretic if not already used)

Not at goal blood pressure

Continue adding agents from other classes;
Consider referral to hypertension specialist

[a]Start with a low dose of a long-acting once-daily drug, and *titrate dose*. Low-dose
combinations may be appropriate.
ACE = angiotensin-converting enzyme; ISA = intrinsic sympathomimetic activity.
Source: Modified from the 6th Report of the Joint National Committee on Prevention,
Detection, Evaluation & Treatment of High Blood Pressure. Arch Intern Med 1997;157:2413.

MANAGEMENT ALGORITHMS: HYPERTENSION

CONSIDERATIONS FOR INDIVIDUALIZING ANTIHYPERTENSIVE DRUG THERAPY

Indication	Drug Therapy
Compelling Indications Unless Contraindicated	
Diabetes mellitus (Type 1) with proteinuria	ACE I
Heart failure	ACE I, diuretics
Isolated systolic hypertension (older patients)	Diuretics (preferred), CA (long-acting DHP)
Myocardial infarctionn	β-blockers (non-ISA), ACE I (with systolic dysfunction)
May Have Favorable Effects on Comorbid Conditions[a]	
Angina	β-blockers, CA
Atrial tachycardia and fibrillation	β-blockers, CA (non-DHP)
Cyclosporine-induced hypertension (caution with the dose of cyclosporine)	CA
Diabetes mellitus (Types 1 and 2) with proteinuria	ACE I (preferred), CA
Diabetes mellitus (Type 2)	Low-dose diuretics
Dyslipidemia	α-Blockers
Essential tremor	β-Blockers (non-CS)
Heart failure	Carvedilol, losartan potassium
Hyperthyroidism	β-Blockers
Migraine	β-Blockers (non-CS), CA (non-DHP)
Myocardial infarction	Diltiazem hydrochloride, verapamil hydrochloride
Osteoporosis	Thiazides
Preoperative hypertension	β-Blockers
Prostatism (BPH)	α-Blockers
Renal insufficiency (caution in renovascular hypertension and creatinine level ≥ 265.2 μmol/L [≥ 3 mg/dL])	ACE I

continued on next page

MANAGEMENT ALGORITHMS: HYPERTENSION

CONSIDERATIONS FOR INDIVIDUALIZING ANTIHYPERTENSIVE DRUG THERAPY (Continued)

Indication	Drug Therapy
May Have Unfavorable Effects on Comorbid Conditions[ab]	
Bronchospastic disease	β-Blockers[c]
Depression	β-Blockers, central α-agonists, reserpine[c]
Diabetes mellitus (types 1 and 2)	β-Blockers, high-dose diuretics
Dyslipidemia	β-Blockers (non-ISA), diuretics (high-dose)
Gout	Diuretics
2° or 3° heart block	β-Blockers,[c] CA (non DHP)[c]
Heart failure	β-Blockers (except carvedilol), CA (except amlodipine besylate; felodipine)
Liver disease	Labetalol hydrochloride, methyldopa[c]
Peripheral vascular disease	β-Blockers
Pregnancy	ACE I,[c] angiotensin II receptor blockers[c]
Renal insufficiency	Potassium-sparing agents
Renovascular disease	ACE I, angiotensin II receptor blockers

ACE I = angiotensin-converting enzyme inhibitors; BPH = benign prostatic hyperplasia; CA = calcium antagonists; DHP = dihydropyridine; ISA = intrinsic sympathomimetic activity; MI = myocardial infarction; non-CS = noncardioselective.

[a]Conditions and drugs are listed in alphabetical order.

[b]These drugs may be used with special monitoring unless contraindicated.

[c]Contraindicated

Source: Adapted from the 6th Report of the Joint National Committee on Prevention, Detection, Evaluation & Treatment of High Blood Pressure. Arch Intern Med 1997;157:2413.

MANAGEMENT ALGORITHMS: PAP SMEAR ABNORMALITIES

ALGORITHM FOR ABNORMAL PAP SMEAR EVALUATION[a]

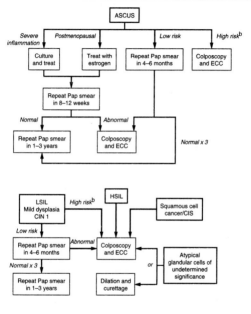

[a]Assumes satisfactory specimen; if unsatisfactory, repeat Pap smear.

[b]High risk = any history of abnormal Pap smear, poor compliance, unlikely to return for follow-up, any human papillomavirus (HPV) changes.

ASCUS = atypical squamous cells of undetermined significance; ECC = endocervical curettage; LSIL = low-grade squamous intraepithelial lesion; CIN = cervical intraepithelial neoplasia; HSIL = high-grade squamous intraepithelial lesion; CIS = carcinoma in situ.

Source: Modified from Rosenfeld JA (editor): Women's Health in Primary Care. Williams & Wilkins, 1997.

PROFESSIONAL SOCIETIES & GOVERNMENTAL AGENCIES

Abbreviation	Full Name	Internet Address
AACE	American Association of Clinical Endocrinologists	www.aace.com
AAD	American Academy of Dermatology	www.aad.org
AAFP	American Academy of Family Physicians	www.aafp.org
AAO	American Academy of Ophthalmology	www.eyenet.org
AAOHNS	American Academy of Otolaryngology/Head & Neck Surgery	www.entnet.org
AAOS	American Academy of Orthopaedic Surgeons	www.aaos.org
AAP	American Academy of Pediatrics	www.aap.org
ACC	American College of Cardiology	www.acc.org
ACCP	American College of Chest Physicians	www.chestnet.org
ACIP	Advisory Committee on Immunization Practices	wonder.cdc.gov
ACOG	American College of Obstetricians and Gynecologists	www.acog.com
ACP	American College of Physicians	www.acponline.org
ACPM	American College of Preventive Medicine	www.acpm.org
ACR	American College of Radiology	www.acr.org
ACS	American Cancer Society	www.cancer.org
ACSM	American College of Sports Medicine	www.acsm.org
ADA	American Diabetes Association	www.diabetes.org
AGA	American Gastroenterological Association	www.gastro.org
AGS	American Geriatrics Society	www.americangeriatrics.org

PROFESSIONAL SOCIETIES & GOVERNMENTAL AGENCIES (CONTINUED)		
AHA	American Heart Association	www.americanheart.org
AHRQ	effective 12/1999 Agency for Healthcare Research and Quality	www.ahcpr.gov
AMA	American Medical Association	www.ama-assn.org
ANA	American Nurses Association	www.nursingworld.org
AOA	American Optometric Association	www.aoanet.org
ASCRS	American Society of Colon and Rectal Surgeons	www.fascrs.org
ASCO	American Society of Clinical Oncology	www.asco.org
ASGE	American Society for Gastrointestinal Endoscopy	www.asge.org
ASHA	American Speech-Language-Hearing Association	www.asha.org
ATA	American Thyroid Association	www.thyroid.org
ATS	American Thoracic Society	www.thoracic.org
AUA	American Urological Association	auanet.org
CDC	Centers for Disease Control and Prevention	www.cdc.gov
CTF	Canadian Task Force on the Periodic Health Examination	www.hc-sc.gc.ca
NCI	National Cancer Institute	cancernet.nci.nih.gov
NEI	National Eye Institute	www.nei.nih.gov
GAPS	Guidelines for Adolescent Preventitive Services	
NHLBI	National Heart, Lung, and Blood Institute	www.nhlbi.nih.gov

PROFESSIONAL SOCIETIES & GOVERNMENTAL AGENCIES (CONTINUED)		
NIDR	National Institute of Dental and Craniofacial Research	www.nidr.nih.gov
NIHCDC	National Institutes of Health Consensus Development Conference	odp.od.nih.gov/consensus/ statements/cdc/cdc.html
NOF	National Osteoporosis Foundation	www.nof.org
NTSB	National Transportation Safety Board	www.ntsb.gov
SCF	Skin Cancer Foundation	www.skincancer.org
SGIM	Society for General Internal Medicine	www.sgim.org
USPSTF	United States Preventive Services Task Force	www.ahcpr.gov/clinic/ uspsfact.htm

REFERENCES

American Academy of Pediatrics and American College of Obstetricians and Gynecologists: Guidelines for Perinatal Care, 4th ed. American College of Obstetricians and Gynecologists, 1997. (referred to as "AAP and ACOG" in Tables)

American College of Obstetricians and Gynecologists: Guidelines for Women's Health Care. American College of Obstetricians and Gynecologists, 1996. (referred to as "ACOG" in Tables)

American College of Physicians: Guide for Adult Immunization, 3rd ed. American College of Physicians, 1994.

The Canadian Task Force on the Periodic Health Examination: The Canadian Guide to Clinical Preventive Health Care. Minister of Public Works and Government Services Canada, 1994. (Referred to as "CTF" in tables.)

The Clinician's Handbook of Preventive Services, 2nd ed. U.S. Public Health Service, International Medical Publishing, Inc., 1998.

Eddy DM: Common Screening Tests. American College of Physicians, 1991.

Elster AB (editor): American Medical Association. AMA Guidelines for Adolescent Preventive Services (GAPS): Recommendations and Rationale. Williams & Wilkins, 1994. (Referred to as "GAPS" in tables.)

Green M (editor): Bright Futures: Guidelines for Health Supervision of Infants, Children, and Adolescents. National Center for Education in Maternal and Child Health, 1994. (Referred to as "Bright Futures" in tables.)

U.S. Preventive Services Task Force: Guide to Clinical Preventive Services, 2nd ed. Williams & Wilkins, 1996. (Referred to as "USP-STF" in tables.)

Index